European Security

European Security

From Ukraine to Washington

Richard Rose

BLOOMSBURY ACADEMIC

LONDON • NEW YORK • OXFORD • NEW DELHI • SYDNEY

BLOOMSBURY ACADEMIC
Bloomsbury Publishing Plc
50 Bedford Square, London, WC1B 3DP, UK
1385 Broadway, New York, NY 10018, USA
29 Earlsfort Terrace, Dublin 2, Ireland

BLOOMSBURY, BLOOMSBURY ACADEMIC and the Diana logo
are trademarks of Bloomsbury Publishing Plc

First published in Great Britain 2025

Professor Richard Rose is the director of the Centre for the Study of Public Policy at the University of Strathclyde Glasgow and a visiting fellow at the Wissenschaftszentrum Berlin and the Robert Schuman Centre of the European University Institute Florence. He has presented seminars in forty-five countries across Europe, the Anglo-American world, Russia and China. Rose's books have been translated into eighteen languages, and he has received a dozen international honours for his contribution to the comparative study of public policy.

Cover design by Anna Perotti @bytheskydesign.com
Cover images © Westend61 & Anna Moneymaker/Getty Images

A catalogue record for this book is available from the British Library.

Library of Congress Cataloging-in-Publication Data
Names: Rose, Richard, 1933- author.
Title: European security : from Ukraine to Washington / Richard Rose.
Description: London ; New York : Bloomsbury Academic, 2025. |
Includes bibliographical references and index.
Identifiers: LCCN 2024026781 (print) | LCCN 2024026782 (ebook) |
ISBN 9781350471306 (hb) | ISBN 9781350471344 (pb) |
ISBN 9781350471337 (epub) | ISBN 9781350471320 (ebook)
Subjects: LCSH: National security–Europe–History. | North Atlantic Treaty Organization–Membership. | European Union–Membership. | European Union countries–Relations–Russia (Federation) | Russia (Federation)–Relations–European Union countries. | Russian Invasion of Ukraine, 2022–Influence.
Classification: LCC UA646 .R667 2025 (print) | LCC UA646 (ebook) |
DDC 355/.03304–dc23/eng/20240924
LC record available at https://lccn.loc.gov/2024026781
LC ebook record available at https://lccn.loc.gov/2024026782

ISBN: HB: 978-1-3504-7130-6
          PB: 978-1-3504-7134-4
          ePDF: 978-1-3504-7132-0
          eBook: 978-1-3504-7133-7

Typeset by Integra Software Services Pvt. Ltd.
Printed and bound in Great Britain

To find out more about our authors and books visit www.bloomsbury.com
and sign up for our newsletters.

Dedication
To my children and grandchildren, may they continue to live
without experiencing war

Contents

Figures

Tables

Preface

The war in Ukraine makes this book immediately relevant while understanding how it challenges European security requires knowledge of the past. Hence, this book starts with the end of the Second World War, when Winston Churchill, Franklin D. Roosevelt and Joseph Stalin met at Yalta to settle the boundaries of Soviet and Western spheres of influence. The result was the division of Europe and the start of the Cold War. The foundation of NATO extended Western Europe's boundaries across the Atlantic as the United States became the prime guarantor of Europe's military security. Concurrently, six European countries created a European Coal and Steel Community that became the grandparent of the European Union.

The fall of the Berlin Wall and the collapse of the Soviet Union extended Europe's boundaries eastward to the Black Sea. The belief spread that even if this was not the end of history, it did end the threat of another war in Europe. The global economy's fluctuations made it appear the major source of insecurity. The European Union's expansion of members and powers offered hope of a new era of European prosperity. As a world power, the United States looked across the Pacific and saw China as a growing economic and military power.

Vladimir Putin's invasion of Ukraine in February 2022 showed that Russian aggression is still a threat to European security. Up to a point, the American government, national governments of Europe and the EU have given financial and military aid to Ukraine since it is seen as fighting a proxy war in defence of the whole of Europe. However, aid does not come in the amount that Ukraine needs. Nor is there agreement about whether aid will continue as long as it takes Ukraine to regain all the territory Russia has seized or just long enough for an armistice that lets Russia keep the Ukrainian territory it has occupied.

The outcome of the 2024 American presidential election will reverberate across Europe to Moscow and Kyiv. If Kamala Harris is elected, Europeans will welcome this as a promise of continuity in the United States underwriting the security of Europe. This book cautions against such unqualified confidence. American interests have long been tilting to the Pacific, and the current polarization of politics shows that a Democrat in the White House can no longer rely on bipartisan Congressional support to fund Europe's defence. Vladimir Putin is counting on a victorious Donald Trump downsizing aid to Ukraine and forcing Kyiv to sue for peace on Moscow's terms. Putin's confidence ignores Trump's unpredictability, rooted in the priority he gives to stating policy in tweets without regard to following through.

Even though fighting continues as this book goes to press, it can deal with challenges that governments from the Black Sea to the Potomac will face once the fighting stops. The threat of further Russian aggression means that Washington must decide whether and how it guarantees Ukraine's future security. In the light of American decisions, European governments must decide what they will do, singly and collectively, to deter Russian aggression. The application of Ukraine to join the European Union challenges the EU to help finance the cost of rebuilding its damaged territory and reform institutions already stretched by its expansion from six to twenty-seven member states. Amidst these changes, the UK government must find where in the world a no-longer-global Britain fits in.

In writing this book I have drawn on the experience of living history forwards, as I am old enough to have been reading newspapers during the Second World War when one didn't know what would happen the next day, let alone after the war ended. Before the fighting in Ukraine stops, I will have been researching problems of European security for seventy years.

Richard Rose
9 August 2024

Security and insecurity

A country's security is greatest when everyone takes it for granted. Up to a point the absence of signs of insecurity, such as bomb damage or rising prices, is evidence of security. However, the security of the country is not a problem that can be solved once and for all. Even when security is high, risks to security have not disappeared: there is simply a low probability of threats to the lives and well-being of a country's population. Maintaining security is a classic responsibility of government that no government can ignore whatever the size of its armed force and its gross domestic product.

Whether a problem is a threat to national security is a political judgement. Since politicians have a preference for good news over bad, there is a tendency to downplay threats. Thus, shortly before the Russian invasion of Ukraine in February 2022, President Emmanuel Macron of France and the German Chancellor Olaf Scholz were having phone conversations with the Kremlin on the assumption that diplomatic negotiations could prevent war. Along the Potomac River in Washington, DC, there was a different perception. The Central Intelligence Agency and the Pentagon released confidential information warning of an imminent Russian invasion of Ukraine. The attack that followed is a reminder that security is contingent not constant.

If a government interprets events as a potential threat to its national security, this creates a crisis demanding a decision. Doing nothing or making ineffectual statements can be temporarily reassuring because it suggests that the threat is not serious. This was the response of European governments to the Russian occupation of Crimea in 2014. Eight years later the Russian invasion of Ukraine created a turning point: the belief that European countries were safe from military attack has been replaced by a sense of insecurity. European governments and the United States are sending military supplies and money to Ukraine because it is fighting a proxy war to defend Europe against Russian aggression.

The traditional meaning of national security is narrow: the safety of a country's population against attack from outside its borders, whether by military force, cyber attacks or the weaponization of energy supplies to create economic insecurity. While individuals feeling threatened by crime can strengthen the locks on their doors, this will not protect them from enemy drones, and working hard to earn more money is a forlorn pursuit if inflation is eroding the value of a country's currency faster than earnings can be spent. People need a government to provide collective protection from threats of war and inflation.

Heads of government have a broad view of security. Problems are raised by ministers of finance and defence, generals and bankers, and there are 24/7 media reports of unwelcome events around the world. In the White House the president spends more time dealing with issues raised by the National Security Council than reading memos from the Council of Economic Advisers. Within this group, advisers specializing in Europe compete for the president's attention with specialists on the Middle East and China and what opinion polls are showing about the president's domestic popularity. In Berlin Olaf Scholz has tried to create a national security council in his office but the move has been frustrated by coalition partners, wanting to keep their influence on security in the hands of the ministries they control. British prime ministers who want to put the economy first cannot ignore unexpected threats to their security from Ukraine. Boris Johnson was quick to gain publicity by flying to Kyiv to show British backing for Ukraine's war effort and divert attention from his behaviour in Downing Street.

To deal with threats to national security from abroad, since the end of the Second World War there has been a growth in multi-national organizations concerned with security. The European Union and the North Atlantic Treaty Organization (NATO) have overlapping but different definitions of security and of Europe. NATO pools military forces of countries reaching across oceans and seas from Turkey to the United States and Canada. Defending economic prosperity is the task of the European Union, with twenty-seven member states extending from the borders of Russia to the Irish Sea. The United Nations and the International Monetary Fund were established with headquarters in New York and Washington, respectively, in order to make it more difficult for the US government to revert to isolationism as it had done after the First World War. Both have global memberships dealing with security: the UN's principal resource is diplomacy and that of the IMF is lending money with conditions attached.

Security fluctuates over time

Neither security nor insecurity is a permanent condition; there are intermittent challenges in the never-ending task of governing. The sequence of activities leading up to a world war takes decades, while the time spent fighting it takes only a few years. For twentieth-century European historians the period spanning two decades after 1919 is an interlude between world wars, while 1945 to 2021 was an era in which war was a problem on distant continents. Annual economic growth needs years of compounding in order to create national prosperity, while a bank crash can happen overnight and lead to years of economic insecurity.

This book shows how European security and insecurity have changed back and forth since the end of the Second World War. The decades that followed, usually referred to as the Cold War era, were actually a period of cold peace and European prosperity. Military security was frozen at a high level guaranteed by two nuclear superpowers on Europe's borders: the United States and the Soviet Union. Economic growth replaced economic insecurity with mass affluence and the creation of a single European market. The unexpected fall of the Berlin Wall restructured security. The Soviet Union's break-up removed the chief military threat to countries on both sides of the Atlantic. The 2008 global recession triggered by a financial crisis in the United States showed that European economies were not as secure in practice as they were in economic theory. Military security began to heat up when Vladimir Putin seized Crimea from Ukraine in 2014, followed by Russia's invasion of Ukraine and global inflation creating insecurity twice over.

Since past events are known, there is an incentive for policymakers to respond to a current threat by doing what worked before. In the words of Georges Clemenceau, French premier during the First World War, 'Generals are always prepared to fight the last war, especially if they have won it'. The German

General Staff, having failed to conquer France in the First World War, learnt a lesson from that defeat and conquered France in the Second World War. Barack Obama, who had seen the United States lose wars in Vietnam and Iraq before he took office, characterized his foreign policy priority as: 'Don't do stupid shit' (Rothkopf, 2014). However, this strongly negative and vague principle leaves open what to do when facing the challenge of military aggression.

While history does not repeat itself, it can rhyme; that is, current events are influenced by legacies from the past. History is embedded in multi-national institutions created after the Second World War to prevent a Third World War breaking out between France and Germany. The United Nations was created in 1945, NATO was founded in 1949 and the European Coal and Steel Community, the grandfather of the European Union, was created in 1951. While each point in time is discrete, they overlap in the minds of policymakers. Vladimir Putin's mind is fixed on the past, when the Soviet Union could rightly claim to be a world power. The mind of Ukrainians is fixed on the present: if they do not succeed in repelling Russian invaders, their country will become a vassal of Moscow. European and American policymakers need to focus on the future: how to defend their national security once the fighting stops and Ukraine seeks membership in NATO and the European Union.

The book's first chapter examines how the end of the Second World War left two non-European superpowers in military control of Europe. Soviet troops in Prague were closer to London than to Moscow, and American troops in Berlin were cheek-by-jowl with Soviet forces while 4,000 miles from Washington. Attempts to hammer out a common Allied policy for the occupation of Germany made clear there was no common policy. The historic centre of Europe, German *Mitteleuropa*, disappeared, bisected by an Iron Curtain separating Eastern and Western Europe.

Wartime allies had different views of peacetime security. Chapter 2 shows how the American government abandoned its traditional policy of avoiding entangling alliances with Europe and became the leader in the collective defence of North Atlantic Europe. When the British government, exhausted by victory, asked the United States to secure the independence of Greece and Turkey in 1947, this extended American engagement to the Black Sea. A new balance of power was established; it was radically different from what had gone before. Instead of European countries providing checks and balances to restrain each other, the two powers on opposite sides of the balance were the United States and the Soviet Union.

European governments began building economic institutions to prevent fighting each other again. The common value they shared was: never again. Chapter 3 explains that their security was initially based on coal and butter. The European Coal and Steel Community, established in 1951, was designed to deprive Germany of essential war materials. The European Economic Community (EEC), established by the Treaty of Rome in 1957, promoted the integration of national markets. It enabled German industry to grow and subsidized French peasants producing butter. Efforts to parallel economic integration by forming a multi-national European Defence Community collapsed in 1954 when the French National Assembly rejected doing so because it would mean re-arming Germany. NATO promptly took on this responsibility. The EEC expanded its economic powers and membership but the admission of the UK weakened the drive towards political integration.

The linchpin of the cold peace disappeared with the bloodless collapse of the Soviet Union after Mikhail Gorbachev unexpectedly became its leader. His aim, as set out in Chapter 4, was to restructure the Soviet Union, and he saw thawing the cold peace as useful to his domestic goals. In a 1987 speech in Prague, Gorbachev spoke of a common European home extending from the Urals to the British Isles. His initiatives won him support from initially sceptical leaders such as Ronald Reagan and Margaret Thatcher. However, they lost him support from Soviet communists. By the end of 1991 both Gorbachev and the Soviet Union were gone, and so was the Iron Curtain.

Across Central and Eastern Europe, governments freed from domination by Moscow sought a return to Europe. The meaning of that term varied with the issue at hand. To secure their national government from again being taken over by a domestic dictator, free competitive elections were immediately held. Although the Soviet Union was gone, the need for security against a military threat remained. Beginning in 1999 ex-communist countries became members of NATO, including three Baltic states that had been forcibly incorporated as republics of the Soviet Union. Joining the European Union promised political security and economic growth. By 2007 ten ex-communist countries were members of the European Union.

In response to the restructuring of Europe, the EEC became the European Union with nominal responsibilities for justice, home and foreign affairs and defence as well as economic security. It also increased the powers of its popularly elected European Parliament to enhance its claims to democratic legitimacy. Chapter 5 shows how the European Union now has many of the characteristics of a state, including a flag, an anthem and a diplomatic service posted in more than 100 countries. However, it continues to lack an armed force that can defend its borders against aggression.

The end of the Cold War brought about a global re-orientation of security priorities. Europe and the United States supported democratization in ex-communist states in the belief that this would improve security, since democracies do not fight each other. The United States sponsored the admission of Russia to the Council of Europe, an assembly of democratic European states, to give a boost to Russian President Boris Yeltsin in his 1996 election campaign. In parallel, European politicians who shared the liberal belief that free trade and mass prosperity promoted national security welcomed the replacement of Soviet-style economies with market economies.

The United States has been pivoting to Asia, the subject of Chapter 6. Although it has never put troops into action to defend a NATO member, in 1950 it did so to defend South Korea against aggression from North Korea. Subsequently, it has sent troops into action in Vietnam, Kuwait, Afghanistan and Iraq. President Richard Nixon's trip to China in 1972 symbolized Washington's tilt to the Pacific. It has been paralleled by a tilt in America's population from the East Coast to the Pacific Coast. In the post-1945 era the main source of immigrants has not been Europe but Latin America and now Asia. California has replaced New York as the most populous American state, and Los Angeles is almost as close to Beijing by air as it is to Berlin. The American commitment to the military security of Europe is now but one part of its role as a global power.

President Vladimir Putin's view of security is a legacy of the Soviet Union; he regards its collapse as one of the great disasters of the twentieth century. As Chapter 7 shows, Putin views Soviet republics that became independent countries as part of Russia's near abroad where it has the right to act to protect itself. When it was occasionally suggested that Ukraine become a NATO member, this idea was dismissed by Washington. After Russian forces occupied two regions of Georgia in 2008, they declared their independence but European countries did not recognize this claim. When Russia seized Crimea, its historic Black Sea naval base, the objections of a corrupt and sometimes pro-Moscow Ukrainian government received little support from Washington. Berlin ignored these military incursions as irrelevant; it profitably maintained economic ties with Russia. It assumed economic interdependence would reduce military insecurity, a strategy summed up in the slogan *Wandel durch Handel* (Change through Trade).

The Russian invasion of Ukraine has created a hot war, but not as before. For Vladimir Putin it is a special military operation. For the United States and its NATO allies, it is a proxy war in which Ukraine is defending the military security of North Atlantic Europe. President Joseph Biden declared it is in America's national interest to prevent the Russian invasion from being successful, and the United States has been the largest provider of military supplies to Ukraine. Chapter 8 shows how the responses of European countries to the war have differed. Finland and Sweden have abandoned reliance on political neutrality and joined NATO. Germany has so far made 90 degrees of its notional 180-degree turn from promoting trade with Russia to defending itself against potential Russian aggression. Poland, with current as well as historic ties with Ukraine, has led NATO in boosting military expenditure and receiving Ukrainian refugees. The EU seeks to protect its members from the damage that the Ukraine war has done to its economy and is co-ordinating aid sent to Ukraine by member states. However, decisions about what and how much money and munitions Ukraine receives are taken by member states in their national interest.

What comes next?

Chapter 9 shifts the focus from the present to the future: What must be done to protect Europe's security once fighting in Ukraine stops? The answer differs by function as well as geography. The Ukrainian government is already working on answers to this question, but what happens depends not only on what Kyiv wants but also on how the war ends and the decisions that other governments take in their own interests.

The American government will be challenged to guarantee the military security of Ukraine. One scenario is that the United States will continue to supply Ukraine with additional war materials to deter or repulse a Russian invasion. However, it will not approve Ukraine's request to join NATO, which would require Congress to approve a treaty committing the United States to go to war with Russia if it once again invaded Ukraine. If Donald Trump becomes president this will be welcomed more in Moscow than in Kyiv. The unreliability of a Trump administration's commitment to Europe's defence will challenge the governments of Europe to develop new and effective means to deter Russian aggression.

The reconstruction of war-damaged Ukraine will take years before its economy can recover from war damage and attain a gross domestic product at the level of neighbouring European countries. There will also be a major need to rebuild housing and infrastructure damaged by the war; this will cost much more than did Marshall Plan aid to post-1945 Western Europe. There is little political appetite in Washington to add hundreds of billions of dollars for post-war reconstruction to what it spends on military aid to Ukraine. Many billions needed for the reconstruction of Ukraine will have to come from Europe and be paid in euros.

Since Ukraine wants to join the European Union this raises big political questions about whether the EU's existing institutions are fit to admit a country as populous and poor as Ukraine. It would upset the balance of policies within the EU since Ukraine gives priority to security. It would also upset the EU's annual expenditure on agriculture and aid for regions because of Ukraine's relatively low standard of living. The requirement of consensus or unanimity in decision-making would be under pressure if enlargement also admitted small West Balkan states with troubled histories and limited political and economic resources.

Whereas continental European countries and the United States have developed new institutions to protect their economic and military security, the UK has been seeking without success to define a new global role since its great power status ended after the Second World War. Chapter 10 shows that its failure to do so reflects both mental and material limitations. Successive prime ministers suffer from post-imperial overstretch: they believe that Britain can simultaneously have a special relationship with the United States, the new

Commonwealth and Europe. There is also a failure to accept that Britain's resources are no longer sufficient for being a global power in competition with superpowers such as the United States and China.

Because every reader is affected by their country's security, this book is written in a style accessible to a wider audience than examiners of a PhD thesis. Clarity of expression takes precedence over technical jargon and unnecessary citations. Internet searches can provide readers with much factual detail, and Google Scholar can lead readers to academic articles that provide far more detail about specific points than there is room for in a single book.

Because security is a prime public policy concern, this book draws on appropriate methods from across the social sciences to analyse threats to European security. It deals with the past as historians do, but not in the same way. To cover changes over most of a century it focuses on major developments. From this perspective the personalities of individual leaders that dominate the media are reduced in size and their intentions are overshadowed by the unintended consequences that follow from their actions. Presenting statistically significant evidence would require a large number of cases irrelevant to Europe, which has had only two major wars in just over a century. The chapters that follow focus on what has substantive consequences for the security of Europe today and tomorrow.

My Oxford doctorate on the foreign policy of the 1945–51 British government involved interviewing ministers who were Washington's reliable European partners in the construction of North Atlantic Europe (Rose, 1960). Research on the American presidency has made clear to me how even the most powerful president is constrained by an international as well as a domestic political system that is stronger than any one politician (Rose, 1991). The fall of the Berlin Wall gave me the opportunity to see how half the peoples of Europe were responding to the transformation of their security and how Russia was different (Rose, 2009). While Britons were debating Brexit, I was researching how the European Union had become part of the domestic politics of European states (Rose, 2015). This book is thus a continuation of a lifelong process of research.

Bibliography

Rose, Charles Richard, 1960. *The Relation of Socialist Principles to British Labour Foreign Policy, 1945–51*. Oxford University, Faculty of Social Studies DPhil. thesis.

Rose, Richard, 1991. *The Postmodern President*. Chatham, NJ: Chatham House, 2nd edition.

Rose, Richard, 2009. *Understanding Post-Communist Transformation*. London: Routledge.

Rose, Richard, 2015. *Representing Europeans: A Pragmatic Approach*. Oxford: Oxford University Press.

Rothkopf, David, 2014. 'Obama's "Don't Do Stupid Shit"'. *Foreign Policy*. https://carnegieendowment.org/2014/06/04/obama-s-don-t-do-stupid-shit-foreign-policy-pub-55817.

Part One

Building a cold peace

1

Victors in search of security

Europeans faced massive problems at the end of the Second World War. For six years the continent had been a battleground; millions of homes and factories had been destroyed and more than 10 million people lost their lives. Money had lost value too; cigarettes and chocolate bars were sometimes used as currencies. People whose houses had lost a roof needed shelter, farmers whose livestock had been slaughtered needed new animals, and returned soldiers and prisoners-of-war needed to regain their health. Those who had temporarily benefitted by backing the Axis lost their property and their reputation. Food was rationed not only in defeated Germany but also in victorious Britain.

Political problems were great. Many regimes were discredited by military defeat and occupation. The politicians and public officials who had served the defeated Axis powers willingly or under duress were too numerous to be deprived of office en masse. However, before citizens of defeated countries could regain control of their government, they had to satisfy occupying powers that they had changed their political direction. Where the American and British armies were strong, this required democratic institutions. In a limited number of states – Norway, Denmark, Belgium and the Netherlands – a democratic constitutional system that had previously existed could be restored. In countries where the Soviet army was dominant, new leaders were either communists or had to co-operate with the political guidance of Moscow.

Whereas the end of the First World War broke up the major empires of Europe, the Second World War broke up the political systems and peoples of Europe. As the next section explains, many political systems were discredited by being on the losing side of the war, and years of occupation by the German army meant that many countries on the winning side contributed little to that victory. The one thing all participants shared was a loss of lives of soldiers and civilians; many millions survived by fleeing their homeland. The following section shows that while the Soviet Union suffered great losses, it also won great spoils in terms of land and resources. By contrast, West European countries that had depended on American military force for their victory were undecided about what followed.

A different Europe than before

There was a widespread consensus among European politicians about what they did not want: the restoration of the political systems that had governed before 1939. The great majority had failed to mitigate the economic insecurity that was widespread almost everywhere, except for Sweden and Nazi Germany. National armies had focused more on domestic security than foreign affairs, and governors valued support by armed force as much as electoral support. In many countries there were parties hoping to take or maintain power by force if necessary; in response, social democratic parties also maintained organized *Schutzbunde* (paramilitary forces).

Democratic and undemocratic regimes. Before the Second World War broke out, European political systems were divided into two groups.

A minority were secure democracies because both governing and opposition parties were committed to democratic institutions. This category included Britain and Scandinavian and Benelux countries. France was an electoral democracy but its democratic parties were challenged by undemocratic forces on both the left and right. Czechoslovakia was the only democratic state in Central Europe, and there were no democracies in Eastern Europe and the Mediterranean.

Undemocratic regimes came in a variety of shapes and sizes. After Poland held its first free election in 1922, it was replaced in 1926 by a military coup led by Marshal Jozef Pilsudski, a nationalist hero; subsequent elections were neither free nor fair. The first Hungarian election was followed by Admiral Miklos Horthy becoming regent with the absolute power of an absent king of Hungary. There were four free elections in Austria in which three parties – Catholic, socialist and pro-German – competed in the streets as well as at the ballot box until the Christian Social government established a dictatorship in 1934. Spain held three democratic elections before a civil war broke out that ended in the victory of the military force of Generalissimo Francisco Franco.

The government of Adolf Hitler that took command of Germany in 1933 was doubly revolutionary. The Nazi government aggressively used paramilitary forces to promote the notional Aryan race of true Germans. It claimed that Germans needed *Lebensraum* (living space) and had a right to take over other countries. The Nazi regime started by annexing Austria and Czechoslovakia before launching the Second World War in Europe with the invasion of Poland in 1939. The fascist dictator of Italy, Benito Mussolini, joined the war in 1940 in the belief that Italy could share in the military spoils that Germany was gaining.

The end of the Second World War left many regimes completely discredited politically because they had been on the losing side (Table 1.1). Hitler's Third Reich, proclaimed to last a thousand years, fell 988 years short of its goal. Mussolini's fascist government was overthrown in 1943 as invading Allied armies were fighting their way up the Italian peninsula, and his successor signed an armistice with the Allied governments. Germany backed a puppet Mussolini regime in northern Italy, and anti-fascist and fascist Italian partisans fought each other until spring 1945. Because Austria was incorporated as a region of the Third Reich, Austrian conscripts fought as members of the German army, principally on the Soviet front.

Three authoritarian East European regimes aligned themselves with Germany in 1940–1 by formally joining the Axis: Bulgaria, Hungary and Romania. Each made claims to Balkan territories that had been assigned neighbouring states after the First World War. Each sent troops to fight alongside the German army on the Soviet front and German troops were also stationed in their country. The antisemitic policies of Germany were enforced

Table 1.1 European states in the Second World War

ALLIES United Kingdom, France, Belgium, Luxembourg, Netherlands, Denmark, Norway, Czechoslovakia, Greece, Yugoslavia, Soviet Union.

AXIS Germany, Austria, Italy, Bulgaria, Hungary, Romania.

INVADED by both Germany and the Soviet Union. Finland, Poland, Estonia, Latvia, Lithuania.

NEUTRAL Sweden, Switzerland, Ireland, Spain, Portugal.

in keeping with national practices. After Stalingrad indicated that Germany would be a big loser, each of the three countries sought to wriggle out of their Axis commitment and negotiate a separate peace. This did not stop the invasion of Soviet troops in pursuit of retreating German armies.

Five countries were invaded by both Soviet and German armies. The Molotov–Ribbentrop Non-Aggression Pact signed in Moscow in August 1939 meant that Germany and the Soviet Union would not fight each other, instead sharing the spoils of war, starting with the invasion of Poland the following month. West European countries declared war on Germany in keeping with their commitment to Poland, but could do nothing to prevent the latter from being occupied by the two aggressors. Subsequently, the allies supported representatives of the Polish government-in-exile in London. The Soviet Union provided a wartime home for Polish communists fleeing German forces.

The Soviet Union invaded Finland in November 1939, and the following spring a peace treaty ceded Finnish territory to the invader. In June 1941, the Finnish government sided with Germany in declaring war on the Soviet Union. After the Soviet Union entered Finland in 1944, the Finnish government agreed an armistice in which it pledged to expel German troops from Finnish territory. In post-war peace treaties, Finland was treated as a co-belligerent with Nazi Germany and gave territory and substantial reparations to the Soviet Union (cf. Kinnunen and Kivimäki, 2012).

The Molotov–Ribbentrop Pact assigned the Baltic states of Estonia, Latvia and Lithuania to the Soviet Union; it occupied all three states in June 1940 and killed or deported opponents to camps in the Soviet Union. In June 1941 the German army seized all three Baltic states when invading the Soviet Union. While some citizens initially welcomed the German forces as liberating their country from Soviet control, experience of German occupiers altered their views. The Soviet Union once again took military command in the final year of the war (Smith, 1996).

Among the eleven European countries classified as Allies, Britain was the only one that was not invaded, albeit major cities were subject to air raids and rocket attacks. The Soviet Union[1] was a major battleground, and Greece

---

[1] To avoid confusion – Soviet successor states that are not in or applying to the European Union, e.g. the Russian Federation, are not included as European countries as that term is used in this book.

and Yugoslavia had internal conflicts between resistance forces as well as being invaded by Italian and German troops. By contrast, most of the West European countries were overwhelmed by the German army with little or no fighting. They surrendered on terms that left much of the administration of their government in the hands of officials who collaborated with German occupation forces, resulting in political and moral damage. France had three wartime governments, the one that surrendered to German control, a collaborationist Vichy regime and a self-proclaimed government-in-exile led by General Charles de Gaulle.

Five countries were able to remain neutral. Sweden and Switzerland had made neutrality a major principle of their security policy before the First World War and backed up their neutrality with well-trained military forces. The Franco regime in Spain pleaded exhaustion from civil war to avoid taking up the German invitation to join the Axis powers. The government of Portugal was formally neutral, but given the military value of its Atlantic islands, acceded to Anglo-American pressure to tilt its neutrality in favour of the Allied side. The government of Ireland, with major issues still unresolved by its war of independence from Britain two decades earlier, was formally neutral while ready to co-operate with British forces to protect its vulnerable coastline.

Dead and displaced peoples. A total war affected a country's civilian population as well as those in battle dress. When cities were bombed or their fields and villages became battlegrounds, people were killed, their work and wages disrupted and there were shortages of food and other necessities. As the end of the war approached, millions fled rather than be liberated by Soviet soldiers; they became displaced persons seeking a new country to live in. Jews were most likely to perish in the Holocaust. An estimated 6 million Jews, more than 90 per cent of the pre-1939 Jewish population of Europe, died at the hands of Nazi Germany and its allies. Given the chaos of war, all these statistics are estimates of the magnitude of death and displacement. The overall pattern is clear: upwards of 10 million European civilians and 10 million military died as a result of the Second World War (Imperial War Museums, 2023).

The most military deaths were suffered by countries that had borne the brunt of the fighting in Europe. The Soviet Union sacrificed the lives of millions of soldiers to stop the German advance deep into its territory. About half of Soviet losses were borne by Russians and one-quarter by Ukrainians. German forces are reckoned to have lost more than 5 million soldiers, the great majority on the Eastern front. Since it was not invaded, the UK lost fewer than 400,000 servicemen, and France, since it surrendered in 1940 and supplied few troops for its liberation by Allied forces, had about 200,000 fighters killed.

Civilian casualties were often greater than military deaths. Poland is an extreme example. Since its armed forces were quickly defeated, they suffered relatively few military deaths, while an estimated 5 million civilians, most of whom were Jewish, died. France suffered more civilian than military deaths by contrast with Britain, whose civilian deaths were less than one-sixth the military death total. The massive number of Soviet military deaths was matched by a similar total of civilian deaths.

Total national deaths depended not only on the size of a country's population but also on the intensity of its military engagement. Thus, the number of German deaths was more than twenty times that of Italy. The fighting in multi-ethnic Yugoslavia was between partisans divided along political and ethnic lines, as well as with German and Italian forces; this made Yugoslavia's death toll of 1 million the third-highest in Europe. The dictatorship of Romania aligned itself with the Axis powers and participated in the invasion of the Soviet Union. That, along with a significant Jewish population, resulted in the country having more than 800,000 deaths, the fourth-highest wartime total of any European country.

At least 40 million people were displaced from their home countries by the war; the overwhelming proportion came from Eastern and Central Europe (Imperial War Museums, 2023). They included millions fleeing from the threats posed by an advancing German or Soviet army, millions who were forcibly deported by occupying armies and millions whose homes had been destroyed by fighting (Imperial War Museums, 2023). In some cases, they were fleeing because where they lived was no longer their homeland but had been taken by another country. An estimated 11 million displaced persons were found in Allied-occupied Germany, including former prisoners of war, released slave labourers and both non-Jewish and Jewish concentration-camp survivors (Antons, 2014).

The great majority of displaced persons did not want to return to where they had come from, as it was no longer the country they had lived in before the Second World War. Soviet citizens and Yugoslavs were particularly fearful of being executed by their post-war government because they had become suspect by becoming refugees. The United Nations Relief and Rehabilitation Agency was established to assist in maintaining refugee camps and organizing the resettlement of refugees in other countries and continents welcoming immigrants.

Soviet security enforced by troops

The Soviet regime was doubly concerned with the security of its communist party-state. It maintained a large domestic surveillance apparatus to suppress potential opposition. Political commissars were attached to military units to ensure that officers followed whatever was the party line and there were party cells within many institutions to keep a watching eye on their official directors. As the Soviet army advanced across Eastern Europe in the final year of the war, there was acceptance among the Allies that East European countries, many of which had sided with Germany, should be within the Soviet sphere of influence. The presence of Soviet troops rather than geography determined the limits of Eastern Europe. Moscow's priority was simple: the integration of these countries under the control of Moscow.

Communist parties were established under the leadership of East European citizens who had taken refuge in Moscow during the war or had resisted national politicians collaborating with Nazi Germany. National parties were joined under Moscow's direction in the Cominform; it had nine members, including communist parties in France, Italy and Yugoslavia. Ideological cleansing disqualified from political participation any deemed unsympathetic to the new role that the Soviet Union would play in their national affairs. To establish pro-Moscow governments, elections were held in which both non-communist as well as communist parties were on the ballot. The elections were competitive but far from fair.

The outcome of competitive elections was not to the full satisfaction of Moscow (see Furtak, 1990; Rose and Munro, 2009). In some countries its Communist Party had to become part of a coalition government. It then turned the coalition into a national front that enabled the communists to govern as a one-party state. In Hungary the Communist Party won only one-sixth of the vote but took control of the Interior Ministry and police. After the 1947 election, it forced the Social Democratic Party to merge with it, and won unanimous support in the 1949 Hungarian election because it was the only party on the ballot. In Romania a grand coalition, including the Communist Party won an overwhelming majority in 1946. After the deposition of the king, it won 93 per cent of the vote in a 1948 election that was fraudulent even by Romanian standards. A Moscow-based Polish Committee of National Liberation was installed as head of a coalition government after Soviet troops occupied Warsaw. In subsequent elections its vote increased as the communist list was the only choice on the ballot to seek votes (Raina, 1990). After the Soviet army took control of Czechoslovakia in March 1945, the following year the Communist Party won a plurality of votes in the Czech lands but not in Slovakia. Following a military coup in February 1948, its list won 89 per cent of the vote; the other 11 per cent was accounted for by voters casting a blank ballot. Elections were held under Soviet rules in Estonia, Latvia and Lithuania that were incorporated as republics of the Soviet Union.

The Warsaw Pact, signed in 1955, institutionalized the military integration of eight communist governments under the control of the Soviet Union. Soviet troops invaded Hungary the following year when the Hungarian government sought to act independently of Moscow. The government was deposed, about 2,500 Hungarians were killed and 200,000 fled to Western Europe. Five Soviet-led Warsaw Pact forces invaded Czechoslovakia during the Prague Spring of 1968 to put down a government seeking to liberalize its communist regime.

Comecon (the Council for Mutual Economic Assistance) was established in 1949 as a Soviet alternative to the Marshall Plan. A primary purpose was to support the Soviet economy rather than assist the economies of the Soviet bloc (Crump and Godard, 2018). Since communist economies were controlled by government planners, Comecon could be used to co-ordinate major economic activities of member states according to political criteria. While the economies of Comecon countries did industrialize and grow, their development did not match the achievements of West European economies, as shown by the striking divergence between the East German command economy and the West German social market economy (Rose, 2009: chapter 3).

The last loophole for civilian flight was closed in 1961 when the Berlin Wall was built and policed by East German guards with orders to shoot to kill anyone who sought to leave the so-called German Democratic Republic. Two years later President John F. Kennedy told the people of West Berlin they were not isolated, proclaiming, 'Ich bin ein Berliner'. The speech confirmed that the commitment of the leader of NATO to the defence of the city was just as firm as that of the Soviet bloc to the defence of East Berliners by its *antifaschistischer Schutzwall* (anti-fascist protective barrier).

Within a decade of the Second World War ending, the Soviet Union had created a bloc of countries that were politically, economically and militarily integrated. They provided a large swathe of countries offering security against another invasion by Germany or NATO powers. The bloc extended much further to the west than any previous Russian empire. East Germany was closer to the West German capital of Bonn than to Warsaw and Prague was well to the west of Vienna. The security zone was further extended by four neutral states – Finland, Sweden, Austria and Switzerland – between the Soviet and NATO blocs of forces.

Deciding what to do with victory

The two great powers when the war ended – the Soviet Union and the United States – were new to their role. Russian tsars had always seen their country engaged with Europe, whether to gain territory, as in the partition of Poland, or as partners in the balance of power that had maintained peace for almost a century after the 1815 Congress of Vienna. The Soviet regime was in a much stronger position than its tsarist predecessors to wield power in Europe, due to the demise of the Habsburg Empire and two successive failures of German regimes to conquer Europe.

The United States was founded by immigrants who rejected Europe. The new country's first president, George Washington, declared in his Farewell Address, 'It is our true policy to steer clear of permanent alliance with any portion of the foreign world'. Thomas Jefferson summarized this view as 'Entangling alliances with none'. This policy was followed until provocative actions by the German government brought American troops to Europe for a brief period of fighting in 1917. Although the United States had participated in the Versailles Conference on the peace of Europe in 1919, it subsequently rejected joining the League of Nations and reverted to an isolationist foreign policy. The engagement of American forces in the Second World War was bigger and longer. However, the American commitment to post-war security was uncertain. The Liberty ships that had carried military supplies to Europe were converted into troop carriers to bring the boys and female auxiliaries back to Peoria and other places far from a troubled Europe.

The UK had survived two world wars without invasion and its institutions remained intact. However, Prime Minister Winston Churchill did not see his country as a European power but as the leader of a global empire. The preservation of that empire was under threat from the Middle East to the Indian sub-continent. To maintain Britain's current needs and future security in uncertain circumstances, Churchill looked across the Atlantic rather than across the English Channel. However, the readiness to maintain the wartime Anglo-American alliance was not reciprocated by Washington. When the British government faced difficulties in maintaining its imperial position, American sympathies tended to be with the colonists. Instead of Britain being given a multi-billion-dollar grant for post-war reconstruction in recognition of its wartime sacrifices, the US Congress voted for a $4 billion loan.

France and Italy, two of the great powers that had contributed to the insecurity of Europe in the 1920s and 1930s, could do little until they had recovered from the stigma of collaboration with the Axis and the trauma of military defeat. The Free French government-in-exile was formed by General Charles de Gaulle in London in June 1940 and became the Provisional Government of the French Republic after the Allies liberated Paris in the summer of 1944. In the first three elections in the new Fourth Republic of France, the French Communist Party won a quarter of the vote, Gaullist parties won a quarter of the vote and centrist parties divided half the vote. A French communist was deputy head of government until the party was excluded from office in 1947 because it was following Moscow's party line.

In Italy a 1946 referendum abolished the monarchy and a constituent assembly created a new republic. The electorate was polarized between a Christian Democratic Party and a left-wing alliance led by the Communist Party of Italy. The Communist Party was excluded from participating in government in 1947 because of its pro-Moscow links. The Christian Democratic Party dominated Italian government for four decades. For almost two decades from the hot autumn (*autonno caldo*) of 1969 to the years of lead (*anni di piombo*), its authority was challenged by extreme left-wing and right-wing groups that used bombings and political assassinations in attempts to destabilize the regime.

The victors had no difficulty in deciding what to do with Germany: it was not allowed to govern itself until new institutions could be put in place to prevent a recurrence of German militarism. Germany was divided into four zones occupied by Soviet, American, British and French forces; Berlin was also divided. In East Germany a communist regime was created in 1949, and in the same year the Federal Republic of Germany was established with its capital in Bonn, a small town in West Germany. Its first election resulted in the formation of a Christian Democratic government and a Social Democratic Party became the official opposition. Anti-democratic parties, including the communists, were marginalized and soon disappeared.

Big Three summits settle boundaries. The leaders of the three great powers were united in wanting to avoid the failure to secure the peace after the First World War. Franklin D. Roosevelt had been an assistant secretary of the navy under President Woodrow Wilson, who thought the First World War would be the war to end all wars. Winston Churchill had been a defence minister during that war and in the 1930s issued clear warnings about the recurrence of war in Europe. Shortly after the 1917 Russian revolution had deposed the tsar, civil war between the Bolsheviks and anti-Bolshevik White Army broke out. Joseph Stalin was a senior Bolshevik official active in combating the anti-Bolshevik forces, which were supported by Polish and British forces. This experience made Stalin regard the Western Allies as a potential threat to the security of a communist USSR.

In December 1943 Stalin, Roosevelt and Churchill met in Tehran to discuss what should happen when the war ended. For Roosevelt and Churchill the immediate priority was a sustained Soviet offensive in Eastern Europe to divide German forces while they launched a second front by landing troops in France. Stalin gained Western endorsement of Soviet territorial aggrandizement, including assigning parts of eastern Poland to Ukraine and parts of eastern Germany to Poland. Roosevelt said he would accept the incorporation of the three Baltic states into the Soviet Union only if their citizens approved this in a referendum. Stalin held a ballot on terms consistent with the Soviet constitution and they approved. In October 1944 Churchill met with Stalin in Moscow and proposed an informal agreement recognizing that Eastern Europe was preponderantly but not exclusively within the Soviet sphere of influence (Resis, 1978).

The three leaders met at the Black Sea resort of Yalta in February 1945 to discuss further measures to achieve security in post-war Europe. For Roosevelt the immediate priority was getting the Soviet Union to enter the war against Japan, in which it had been neutral, by attacking its Asian border. For Churchill a major priority was that the governments of the liberated countries of Eastern Europe, especially Poland, would be established by free elections. With Soviet troops less than a hundred miles from Berlin, Stalin reaffirmed that his position was to keep troops there. The initial British and American view was to see this as seeking Russian security rather than as a strategy to impose communist regimes (Miller, 2020: 74). There was a readiness to consider that Germany, which had only become united as a state through a late-nineteenth-century process of amalgamating territories, could be broken up into multiple states to prevent it from regaining the military capacity of the Prussian Empire or the Third Reich.

When the three leaders met again at Potsdam in July 1945, the war in Europe had ended but the terms of a peace settlement had yet to be secured. The president of the United States was now Harry Truman, as Roosevelt had died a month before the war ended. In the middle of the conference, Winston Churchill learnt that he was no longer prime minister when his party was roundly defeated in a British general election. The new Labour prime minister was Clement Attlee; he and his foreign secretary, Ernest Bevin, became senior ministers in the British War Cabinet in 1940, when the country was suffering Germany's air offensive and the Soviet Union was digesting the territorial fruits of the Molotov–Ribbentrop Pact.

At Potsdam the victors agreed on the demilitarization and division of Germany into separate zones occupied by the victors. Its eastern border was moved west to the Oder–Neisse rivers. This reduced German territory by approximately one-quarter from its pre–Second World War boundaries and by one-third from its 1913 boundaries. The territories lost were gained by Poland. Ethnic Germans, many resident in these territories for centuries, were meant to return to Germany by what the Conference protocol described as 'orderly and humane methods' (https://avalon.law.yale.edu/20th_century/decade17.asp). Estimates of the number of displaced Germans who died in the process vary around 1 million people. The Soviet Union was authorized to seize as reparations German industrial equipment far superior to what the Soviet Union produced. German industries that could make war materials, such as chemical factories, steel works and shipyards, were to be dismantled or reduced in size.

The three heads of state agreed to create a Council of Foreign Ministers to produce a peace treaty specifying how principles agreed at Potsdam would be implemented and determining the status of belligerents such as Austria and Italy. The Council's membership was expanded to include France and its secretariat located in London. The Council's effort to put these general discussions into binding treaties showed that the Soviet Union's approach to Europe differed from the United States and Britain. The presence of Soviet troops across Eastern and much of Central Europe gave de facto recognition to Stalin's claim to a Soviet sphere of influence.

The major institution that emerged from great-power talks was not European but global, the United Nations. Creating it was a major goal of Franklin Roosevelt. Given that the United States was fighting a war in Asia as well as Europe, the global focus was appropriate. Roosevelt saw the Soviet Union's participation in the United Nations as essential and used face-to-face meetings with Stalin to encourage his commitment. In the summer of 1944 a seven-week conference of high-level representatives of the Soviet Union, the United Kingdom and the United States met at Dumbarton Oaks in Washington to draft the terms of an International Peace and Security Organisation. The Nationalist Chinese government participated in the final week.

The conference proposed a two-tier structure: a General Assembly of countries from all continents regardless of their economic and political weight, and a Security Council, in which great powers would be permanent members and each would have a veto. The assembly's inclusiveness was necessary for the United Nations to deal with global economic and social problems wherever they occurred. The Security Council was necessary for great powers to be able to veto proposals that they considered inconsistent with their own national security. The details of the United Nations Charter were drafted at a lengthy founding conference of forty-four countries; it was meeting in San Francisco the day the war in Europe ended.

From a European perspective the principles of the United Nations were acceptable, and most European countries were founder-members of the UN when it was established in October 1945. However, the UN was redundant for meeting challenges facing European states. If they agreed on a security issue, they did not need to have their decisions endorsed by the Security Council. If they disagreed, then a veto by a European member of the Council would prevent the UN from adopting a policy. After experiencing two wars in which differences were decided by armed force, European governments saw security as requiring the one thing the United Nations did not have, a military force to deter a potential aggressor. This need was met by the creation of a multi-national military force with the power of command located not in Europe but in Washington.

Bibliography

Antons, Jan-Hinnerk, 2014. 'Displaced Persons in Post-War Germany'. *Journal of Contemporary History*, 49, 1, 92–114.

Crump, Laurien and Godard, Simon, 2018. 'Reassessing Communist International Organisations'. *Contemporary European History*, 27, 1, 85–109.

Furtak, Robert, ed., 1990. *Elections in Socialist States*. London: Harvester Press.

Imperial War Museums, 2023. 'What Happened to People Displaced by the Second World War?'. London. iwm.org.uk/history/what-happened-to-people-displaced-by-the-second-world-war#. Accessed 6 August 2023.

Kinnunen, Tiina and Kivimäki, Ville, eds., 2012. *Finland in World War II: History, Memory, Interpretations*. Leiden: Brill.

Miller, Benjamin, 2020. *Grand Strategy from Truman to Trump*. Chicago: University of Chicago Press.

Raina, Peter, 1990. 'Elections in Poland'. In Robert Furtak, ed., *Elections in Socialist States*, London: Harvester Press, 98–118.

Resis, Albert, 1978. 'The Churchill–Stalin Secret Percentages Agreement on the Balkans, Moscow, October 1944'. *American Historical Review*, 83, 2, 368–87.

Rose, Richard, 2009. *Understanding Post-Communist Transformation: A Bottom Up Approach*. London: Routledge.

Rose, Richard and Munro, Neil, 2009. *Parties and Elections in New European Democracies*. Colchester: ECPR Press.

Smith, Graham, ed., 1996. *The Baltic States: The National Self-Determination of Estonia, Latvia and Lithuania*. London: Palgrave Macmillan.

2

Building a North Atlantic Europe

Victory in Europe did not mean the end of the Second World War for the American government. The war in the Pacific was still a hot war, and the United States faced the prospect of the massive loss of American troops in invading Japan. The dropping of two American atomic bombs on Japan in August 1945 led to Japan's immediate surrender without a further fight (Frank, 1999). A Japanese government remained in place under Emperor Hirohito, who was subject to General Douglas MacArthur, the American Supreme Commander of occupying forces. The Soviet Union, which had entered the war in its closing weeks, refused to participate in the occupation in a position subordinate to MacArthur. The new Japanese government administered the country's reconstruction and development, while American troops maintained security.

In Europe the United States faced the challenge of achieving post-war security by a settlement that would not become a prelude to another world war. The Soviet Union as well as the United States was an occupying power, the governments and boundaries of much of Europe were disrupted, and the Soviet manner of achieving its own security gave cause for insecurity in other countries. There was an unstable relationship between victorious allies and uncertainty about the political situation in many countries that had been occupied.

The fundamental issue was whether it was in the American national interest to remain directly engaged in Europe and, if so, how? The new president, Harry Truman, as a senator had promoted the efficient domestic mobilization of war materials but was out of the foreign policy loop. Soviet agents were providing Joseph Stalin with more information about critical American policies than Truman received as vice president. While Truman's mind was fresh to foreign affairs, it was not empty. From his youth he had been an omnivorous reader of history, and as a captain of an anti-artillery brigade in France in the First World War, he had seen war on the ground. Moreover, in the Senate he was accustomed to the process of bargaining to achieve a policy consensus. Truman had a more realistic view of security than the liberal optimism of his predecessor, Franklin D. Roosevelt.

Up to a point, the military force and economic strength of the United States made it the dominant force in Western Europe, as the next section shows. However, its position was limited geographically and the Soviet Union was very much the hegemon in Eastern Europe. The American monopoly of nuclear weapons was limited in time, since the USSR was racing to develop its own nuclear weapons. To be an effective hegemon from a base on the Potomac, the American government needed the participation of the countries it was defending. However, the end of the war left most countries with limited resources. The second section sets out how the United States provided substantial economic aid through the Marshall Plan and support for military security through the Truman Doctrine, deterring Soviet aggression in Greece and Turkey. The concluding section describes how four years after the end of the Second World War, the North Atlantic Treaty Organization (NATO) was established to defend collective security from the Potomac to the Black Sea.

Deterring a Third World War

The ancient Romans understood the logic of armaments as a source of peace: *Si vis pacem, para bellum* (If you want peace, prepare for war). Nineteenth-century European governments applied this principle in efforts to maintain a balance of power in which no country had sufficient arms to dominate Europe. This was achieved through mutual-defence alliances between groups of countries that each had substantial military forces. However, the balance was not always effective. Alliances triggered the First World War between the Central Powers (Germany, the Austro-Hungarian Empire and the Ottoman Empire) and the Triple Entente of France, the UK and the Russian tsar.

Until the outbreak of the Second World War, the United States rejected joining an alliance to maintain its national security. The Atlantic Ocean was regarded as a sufficient deterrent to a European conflagration reaching it.

Liberal idealists such as Andrew Carnegie promoted peacemaking measures on the theory *Si vis pacem, para pactum* ('If you want peace, agree to keep the peace'). To this end, he founded the Carnegie Endowment for International Peace in 1910 to encourage co-operation between nations and American engagement in international affairs. American isolationists did not need a knowledge of Latin to promote their view: if you want peace, stay out of Europe.

Deterrence in theory and practice. To prevent military conflict with Soviet Russia the United States applied the theory of deterrence: the prevention of war by making a potential attacker fear the consequences (Schelling, 1966). To be effective, a policy of deterrence requires a government to have the military capacity to inflict certain and severe damage on a potential aggressor that could launch a military attack. In a philosophical sense it is not possible to be certain about future actions, but deterrence strategy assumes that potential aggressors will be put off if they realized what could happen to them if they did make an armed attack.

When the Second World War ended, the United States had a unique deterrent: the atomic bomb. Since atomic weapons were not the sole source of American military power, the American government endorsed the principle of the control and non-proliferation of nuclear weapons. It supported the 1946 resolution of the United Nations General Assembly for the establishment of the United Nations Atomic Energy Commission to promote the peaceful use of nuclear power and eliminate nuclear weapons from national forces by effective safeguards against violation. Effectiveness was to be secured by removing the right of permanent members of the Security Council to veto enforcement measures. The plan was endorsed by the Atomic Energy Commission but not adopted because the Soviet Union was unwilling to give up its veto.

Deterrence produced an arms race. The Soviet Union began working on nuclear weapons in 1946, making use of information obtained from communist spies participating in the American project. By 1949 it was able to produce atomic bombs. To maintain its lead, the United States began working on hydrogen power and exploded its first hydrogen bomb in 1952. The Soviet Union exploded its first hydrogen bomb three years later. Each country then proceeded to build a stockpile of nuclear weapons and develop the capacity to deliver atomic bombs by planes, missiles and submarines. This gave both the

United States and the Soviet Union enough second-strike capability to respond to a destructive attack by imposing a similar level of destruction on the other. This system of mutually assured destruction, with the acronym MAD, showed that it would be insane for a country to launch a nuclear attack if it knew in advance that doing so would result in its own destruction.

The escalation in the power of nuclear weapons left open the risk that, if only by accident, they could be used and trigger another global war. It also imposed significant costs on national resources. Months after the Cuban missile crisis created an unplanned and potentially explosive confrontation between the two great nuclear powers, President John F. Kennedy proposed a de-escalation in the nuclear arms race. The United States would stop tests of nuclear weapons if other countries did so. In 1968 a Nuclear Non-Proliferation Treaty won global support; it proposed limiting nuclear weapons to the countries that were the five permanent members of the UN Security Council. President Richard Nixon followed up with a Strategic Arms Limitation Treaty with the Soviet Union.

While all European countries had an interest in deterring a Third World War, the dynamics of nuclear deterrence took place over their heads. The protagonists – the United States and the Soviet Union – were on other continents. The two European countries with nuclear weapons, the UK and France, were marginal actors. Britain relied on the United States for technology and equipment essential to maintain its fleet of nuclear submarines. France lacked the resources to use its nuclear weapons in a direct confrontation with another great power. Moreover, European countries accustomed to being the battleground for armed conflicts had no wish to see their densely populated lands become the site of a nuclear war.

Foundations of a secure Europe

The end of the Second World War settled the boundaries of a divided Europe. Soviet Europe consisted of those countries in which the presence of Soviet troops had created new national governments. By the end of the 1940s they were linked to Moscow politically, economically and militarily (see Section 1.2). Free Europe, that is, countries free of domination by Moscow, were initially a residual category of diverse countries. Geographically, it extended from Scandinavia to Greece and in the west to Ireland. The category included countries on opposing sides in the Second World War and neutral countries, countries with new political regimes and those with old institutions and governments chosen by free elections or without any elections. There were also substantial differences in economic conditions among the countries of free Europe.

Political continuity and discontinuity. Among the European countries with political systems that had survived the Second World War, eight had governed continuously since before the First World War. In addition, four regimes were created in the aftermath of the First World War; two were democracies – Ireland and Finland – and three were undemocratic – Turkey, Spain and Portugal.

The regimes of the Axis Powers were repudiated by defeat. In 1946 neither Germany nor Austria was an independent country; both were subject to four-power occupation by the victors. The three Allied zones of Germany were transferred to the demilitarized Federal Republic of Germany in 1949. Although Austria had held free elections in 1945, it gained freedom from four-power occupation only in 1955 on terms that required it to abstain from military alignment with NATO or the Warsaw Pact. Franco Spain's regime was stable up to a point, since authority was vested in Franco personally. It dissolved peacefully after his death in 1975. Greece had entered the Second World War as a monarchical regime with a dictatorship; governments chosen by free elections after the war fell to a military coup in 1967.

In France and Italy free elections showed significant divisions between parties that welcomed being part of free Europe and those that favoured the Soviet Union. It took two referendums in France before a Fourth Republic could be authorized to replace the authoritarian Vichy regime. It collapsed within twelve years. In Italy the new Republican regime was stable after a fashion due to polarization between communist and anti-communist parties; this lasted until the Soviet Union broke up. However, control of government was chronically unstable as opportunism and intrigues within the anti-communist coalition resulted in the average Italian prime minister lasting less than a year in office.

Political discontinuities left the United States with the responsibility of defending free Europe against Soviet ambitions to expand. Within Germany there was left-wing opposition to rearmament, and in countries that Nazi Germany had occupied significant opposition to the idea of German rearmament. In France Gaullists did not want to accept a position subordinate to American forces, communists were inclined to favour the Soviet Union, and centrists saw the value of allying with the United States. The Italian experience of being on both the losing side and a battleground in the Second World War created a popular distaste for the use of force. Only the British Labour government consistently supported the United States protecting European security, as victory had weakened the UK economically and its military resources were strained by policing an increasingly fractious empire on other continents.

Economic recovery. During the 1930s European economies were affected by the world depression, although they did not have modern, industrialized economies on the scale of the United Kingdom and the United States. During the Second World War the Blitz of Britain subjected major British cities to German bombing. Allied bombing of Germany laid waste to Europe's largest industrial economy and destroyed rail services that made it difficult to distribute food supplies. Occupied countries such as France, which had a larger peasant than industrial population, were able to cushion the destruction of war by relying on a traditional rural economy (Franklin, 1969). What Europe needed in 1945 was to repair wartime destruction and to make major reforms so that economic recovery would be followed by economic growth.

The immediate problem was to cope with wartime destruction that had caused post-war agricultural and industrial output to fall below 1938 levels. Inflation produced a surplus of paper money; goods and services could be bartered rather than sold. Food was in short supply due to unfavourable weather conditions. Where food was rationed at a level only a little above minimum calorie requirements, black markets sprang up. The United States provided millions of tonnes of food supplies, especially grain for making bread. The United Nations Relief and Rehabilitation Agency (UNRRA) financed $3.7 billion worth of food, clothing, tools and other basic necessities; two-thirds of that cost was met by the United States.

Because Germany had used its industrial prowess to build modern weapons of war, the victorious powers initially sought the industrial disarmament of Germany, due to a fear that rebuilding its heavy industry would support a revived German military force. Under the terms of peace treaties, the Soviet Union was allowed to remove masses of industrial equipment for use in restoring and upgrading its own economy. When the American government realized that European economic recovery could make little progress without the recovery of German industry, the policy was reversed (Beschloss, 2003).

Policymakers in Europe and Washington agreed upon the need for American aid to achieve the economic reform of Europe so that it could achieve military security (Leffler, 1998). President Truman endorsed the State Department proposals for American economic assistance. Because the Republican Party controlled Congress, the State Department consulted Arthur Vandenberg, the chairman of the Senate Committee on Foreign Relations (Haas, 2016).

The economic recovery programme became known as the Marshall Plan, because it was publicly launched by Secretary of State George Marshall in a speech at Harvard on 5 June 1947. It proposed replacing the ad hoc flow of more than $10 billion American aid with a co-ordinated programme to rebuild war-torn regions, modernize industry and remove trade barriers between European countries. It emphasized that, as a condition of receiving American aid, Europeans would need to co-operate with each other in deciding how much money each country received and how it should be spent. Marshall's speech avoided any reference to military security. By prior arrangement, Britain and France called a meeting in Paris of European countries to discuss the proposed recovery programme. The Soviet Union was invited but rejected participating in an American-sponsored programme, and Soviet satellite countries that wanted to participate were forbidden to do so by Moscow.

The Committee of European Economic Co-operation was established to act on behalf of European countries sharing in American assistance. It initially had sixteen members, eight countries that had been wartime allies, six neutral countries and two former enemies. After it gained a government of its own, Germany joined. The United States established a parallel Economic Cooperation Administration to facilitate the delivery of aid.

The preamble of the Act of Congress that authorized the Marshall Plan justified spending billions of American dollars in Europe as supporting the strength and stability of the United States. The bill received approval from big majorities in both the House and the Senate. Only seventeen senators and seventy-one members of the House of Representatives, mostly Republicans, voted against it. The act authorized expenditure on essential commodities such as food and raw materials; upgrading industrial, transportation and communications equipment; technical assistance; American experts and visits of European producers to learn how the American market economy worked. American grants of $13 billion were multiplied by counterpart funds that European recipients were expected to spend in their national currency on related recovery and modernization projects. The major recipients of funds were the UK, 26 per cent; France, 18 per cent; and Germany, 11 per cent.

By the time the Marshall Aid programme stopped, the per capita gross national product of Western Europe had grown by 33 per cent. The political effects were incalculable but substantial, since economic growth increased the political stability of free nations and their readiness to co-operate with the United States. It also boosted American industries that were the principal suppliers of goods that the recipient countries imported (Hitchcock, 2010; Hogan, 1987; Milward, 1984).

Military containment. The end of the Second World War left masses of American troops on the ground in the defeated countries of Central Europe. As long as they remained in place there was an immediate barrier to Soviet troops continuing their advance to the Atlantic Ocean, and the end of the war meant that the United States no longer needed to give uncritical support to the Soviet Union. Soviet actions during and immediately after the war had raised suspicions of Soviet intentions. However, the United States lacked a strategy to deal with the Soviet Union.

George Kennan, a State Department expert, set out a strategy to contain the Soviet Union in the American national interest, in a long telegram sent from the Moscow Embassy to the secretary of state in February 1946. Kennan wrote that military victory had left the Soviet Union overextended across Eastern Europe but also insecure in the light of the penetration of German troops into Soviet territory as far east as Stalingrad. The country was therefore seeking to increase its security by establishing a series of satellite communist states in Eastern Europe. Accepting this as a *fait accompli*, Kennan (1947) recommended that the United States should be on guard against Soviet attempts to take advantage of the military and economic weakness of Europe's states to extend its borders westward.

Writing under the pseudonym X, Kennan gave the name 'containment' to the strategy he advocated: 'It is clear that the main element of any United States policy toward the Soviet Union must be that of long-term, patient but firm and vigilant containment of Russian expansive tendencies.' He saw containment maintained through diplomatic means and by giving economic aid to European countries that had suffered wartime destruction, thereby making them readier to ally with the United States in resisting the USSR's efforts. He rejected the idea of relying primarily on military force, believing that this would create an arms race by heightening the Kremlin's feeling of being threatened by the armed strength of a foreign power. Kennan's recommendation to contain Soviet expansion was accepted, but his rejection of creating a massive military force to balance the Soviet Union was not.

At the time Kennan wrote, there were threats of communist takeovers in Mediterranean Europe. In Yugoslavia a wartime split in resistance to German occupation ended with the victory of Josip Tito's multi-ethnic communist partisans over pro-royalist forces. The Tito government then aligned itself with the Soviet bloc. In Greece pro-monarchist and communist resistance groups had fought each other as well as German occupation forces. After Athens was taken by British forces and a Greek exile army, an anti-communist government was formed. It was challenged by communist forces in a brutal civil war. Since Stalin kept to his agreement with Churchill that Greece was in the British sphere of influence, the Greek communists received little support from Moscow. The civil war temporarily stopped in February 1945, only to break out again in March 1946. The UK continued to be the chief Allied supporter of the anti-communist Greek government. It provided tens of millions of pounds in economic assistance and stationed more than 3,000 British troops there.

Turkey had remained neutral during the Second World War. In August 1946, the Soviet Union notified Turkey that it wanted a revision of the Montreux Treaty to allow its warships access to the Mediterranean. This was followed by intimidating a Turkish government that was no match for Soviet troops in Bulgaria, which had a land border with Turkey. Its warships patrolled Black Sea waters near the Turkish Straits. An alarmed Turkish government turned to the United States for support.

The British government gave notice to Washington on 21 February 1947 that it was withdrawing its support for the Greek and Turkish governments as its financial resources were overstretched domestically by demands for independence in India and by its mandate to govern Palestine (Bilgin and Morewood, 2004; Frazier, 1984; Jones, 1955). In an address to Congress a few weeks later, President Truman announced what became known as the Truman Doctrine. It stated that the United States would protect foreign governments facing 'subjugation by armed minorities or by outside pressures', a barely coded reference to the Greek civil war and Soviet pressure on Turkey. When seeking congressional support for giving $400 million in economic and military aid to Greece and Turkey, Secretary of State Dean Acheson set out what became known as the domino theory. He postulated that if even a single country allied to the United States fell to an unfriendly power, it would be followed by the fall of many more countries.

When a Republican-controlled Congress endorsed Truman's request for aid to Greece and Turkey, this marked the beginning of decades of bipartisan support for extending the protection of American security from the Potomac to the Black Sea. As the Soviet Union had no troops in Greece or Turkey, the Kremlin accepted that the two countries were now in the American sphere of influence. While the Truman Doctrine was important in implementing the idea of containment, it was a statement of principles rather than a treaty committing American troops to come to the aid of Greece or Turkey if either as invaded by Soviet troops.

The Berlin airlift that began the following year as an Allied response to a Soviet attempt to blockade Allied sectors of the city, which was an isolated island geographically within Soviet-controlled East Germany. On 24 June 1948 the Soviet authorities abruptly suspended all access to Berlin by road and rail from West Germany, the route by which Berliners in Allied sectors of the city received daily shipments of food and goods vital for their survival. This had the boomerang effect of prompting the non-violent use of force to implement the Truman Doctrine (US State Department, 2023). Within forty-eight hours the US Air Force, backed by the British, began airlifting supplies to Berlin, landing at airports that were within the Allied sectors of the city. Sufficient planes were mobilized to transport the coal needed to supply electricity and heat during the cold winter that followed. At the height of the airlift, one plane with supplies landed every forty-five seconds. Eleven months later the Soviet administration abandoned its blockade.

NATO: Containing force with force

Commitment to deterrence did not stipulate under what circumstances the United States would respond to Soviet military actions and which countries it would be prepared to go to war to defend. It had only gone to war in Europe when directly attacked by Germany in 1917 and 1941. However, if the USSR attacked a free country in Europe, Soviet troops would not necessarily engage with American forces in Germany and Austria. To make deterrence a clearly defined threat, the White House had to clarify for which countries it would go to war to halt Soviet troops and European governments had to decide whether they wanted to rely on American military protection.

Britain and France took the initiative in formalizing an agreement to come to the defence of the other in 1947. The following year a Treaty added the commitment of Belgium, Luxembourg and the Netherlands to mutual defence if any of the others was attacked. Their joint commitment fell short of being an effective deterrence to Soviet forces in the absence of an American commitment to do the same. While President Truman understood their need, he was cautious about proceeding, since it could pre-empt the constitutional power of the US Congress to declare war. Bipartisan endorsement was crucial, because negotiations for a treaty would only conclude after an autumn election that was widely expected to be won by a Republican candidate. After discussions with the State Department, Senator Arthur Vandenberg offered to introduce a resolution that would authorize President Truman to negotiate a treaty with European countries that would offer them military assistance on terms subject to American constitutional processes. In June a non-binding resolution was approved by a bipartisan vote, with only thirteen senators opposing.

Negotiations between Washington and West European countries required resolving major differences of opinion. The Brussels Treaty countries preferred that the alliance was limited to themselves, while Washington wanted to include countries bordering the North Atlantic from Portugal to Iceland, as they were strategically far more important in ensuring American military access to the European continent than Benelux countries and France. The European countries sought military aid in the form of bilateral links, while the United States insisted on creating an institution to provide collective defence.

Washington negotiators also made clear that approval of a treaty by the US Senate had to take the Vandenberg Resolution into account.

The North Atlantic Treaty for mutual defence assistance was signed in April 1949. Article 5 was phrased to meet the concerns of Congress. It stated that an armed attack against one or more signer would be considered an attack against all of them and that each signer would respond by taking such action as it deemed necessary, including the use of armed force. The colonial territories of the signers were excluded from collective defence. The treaty also made provision for military aid and co-operation through a North Atlantic Treaty Organization. After ten days of debate, the US Senate approved the treaty by a bipartisan vote of eighty-two to thirteen. Richard Nixon, then a senator from California, abstained. Although the treaty had been negotiated by a State Department led by an Ivy League elite, it was endorsed by senators representing states from coast to coast. Nine of the senators voting against the NATO Treaty represented states that Donald Trump subsequently carried in 2016 and 2020.

Even though Korea was geographically remote from Europe and the United States, the North Korean invasion of the Republic of Korea in 1950 had a double impact on NATO. The prompt response of President Truman to commit American troops to defend a distant Asian state offered practical evidence that the White House would support European countries if attacked. Six NATO members besides the United States sent troops to Korea, and two more sent hospital units. Greece and Turkey also sent troops and were admitted to NATO while the fighting was going on.

In December 1950 General Dwight D. Eisenhower, who had led Allied troops in the liberation of Western Europe, was named NATO's first Supreme Allied Commander Europe (SACEUR) to co-ordinate member-state forces for mutual defence. It was not until two years later that a NATO secretary-general was appointed, Lord Ismay, the chief military assistant to Winston Churchill in the Second World War. When Eisenhower became president of the United States, he appointed as his secretary of state John Foster Dulles, who had espoused policies of rolling back Soviet power and liberating Eastern Europe from Moscow's control. However, when the Hungarian government peacefully sought independence from Moscow at the end of the first term of the Eisenhower administration, consistent with the doctrine of containment, the United States stood by while Soviet troops crushed Hungarian insurgents.

Table 2.1 Cold War Europe in 1955

NATO members, 15: Norway, Denmark, the Netherlands, Belgium, Luxembourg, West Germany, France, the United Kingdom, Italy, Portugal, Greece, Turkey, Canada, Iceland and the United States.

Neutral and free, 5: Ireland, Spain, Austria, Switzerland and Finland.

Soviet bloc, 10: East Germany, Czechoslovakia, Hungary, Poland, Bulgaria, Romania, and the Soviet Union including Estonia, Latvia and Lithuania.

Other, 2: Albania and Yugoslavia.

Source: Author.

The creation of NATO meant that there was a North Atlantic force to deter Soviet aggression from the Potomac to the Black Sea (Table 2.1). In addition to the United States, the leading military forces were those of Turkey and the United Kingdom. French forces were occupied with a colonial war in Algeria. The accession of Germany to NATO in 1955 after a failed attempt to create a strictly European Defence Community (see Section 3.1) brought the borders of NATO up to the Iron Curtain. The establishment of a Cold War boundary patrolled by NATO troops satisfied the hunger of European leaders for military security. However, the ending of Marshall Plan aid in 1952 left European recipients to fend for themselves in seeking prosperity as well as peace.

Bibliography

Beschloss, Michael R., 2003. *The Conquerors: Roosevelt, Truman and the Destruction of Hitler's Germany, 1941–1945*. New York: Simon & Schuster.

Bilgin, Mustafa Sitki and Morewood, Steven, 2004. 'Turkey's Reliance on Britain: 1943–1947'. *Middle Eastern Studies*, 40, 2, 24–57.

Frank, Richard, 1999. *Downfall: The End of the Imperial Japanese Empire*. New York: Random House.

Franklin, S. H., 1969. *The European Peasantry: The Final Phase*. London: Methuen.

Frazier, Robert, 1984. 'Did Britain Start the Cold War? Bevin and the Truman Doctrine'. *Historical Journal*, 27, 3, 715–27.

Haas, Larry J., 2016. *Harry & Arthur: Truman, Vandenberg, and the Partnership That Created the Free World*. Washington, DC: Potomac Books.

Hitchcock, William, 2010. 'The Marshall Plan and the Creation of the West'. In Melvin P. Leffler and Odd A. Westad, eds., *The Cambridge History of the Cold War*, 3 vols. Cambridge: Cambridge University Press, vol. I, 154–74.

Hogan, Michael J., 1987. *The Marshall Plan: America, Britain and the Reconstruction of the Western Europe, 1947–1952*. Cambridge: Cambridge University Press.

Jones, Joseph M., 1955. *The Fifteen Weeks*. New York: Viking Press.

Kennan, George F., 1947. 'The Sources of Soviet Conduct'. *Foreign Affairs*, 25, 4, 561–82.

Leffler, Melvyn P., 1998. 'The United States and the Strategic Dimensions of the Marshall Plan'. *Diplomatic History*, 12, 3, 277–306

Milward, Alan, 1984. *The Reconstruction of Western Europe, 1945–1951*. London: Methuen.

Schelling, Thomas C., 1966. *Arms and Influence*. New Haven: Yale University Press.

US State Department, 2023. 'The Berlin Airlift, 1948–1949'. history.state.gov/milestones/1945-1952/berlin-airlift. Accessed 10 August 2023.

3

Building European security without guns

European leaders shared a common goal at the end of the Second World War: never again. The question was: How to prevent another war? Two European wars in a lifetime showed political leaders that national sovereignty did not guarantee military security. After what H. G. Wells called 'the war to end wars', Allied victors spent a decade trying to hold down Germany's democratic Weimar Republic and more years trying to appease Adolf Hitler's Third Reich. National governments tried to secure economic prosperity independent of other national economies. The world depression showed that nationalist economic policies did not provide economic security. These failures created a demand for European institutions that would prevent a Third World War.

There was vocal support for the creation of a vaguely defined United States of Europe, but no agreement about what this represented in practice or how to achieve it. Before the war was over, Altiero Spinelli, an imprisoned Italian anti-fascist, wrote a manifesto calling for a federal union among European peoples, and a Union of European Federalists was created in 1946. There was disagreement within the movement between those who pushed for the creation of a union with the powers of a federal state and those who favoured piecemeal progress through European institutions dealing with specific economic and political functions (Mayne, Pinder and Roberts, 1990).

Concurrently, Winston Churchill, then in opposition in the British Parliament, endorsed a United States of Europe in a 1946 Zurich speech. It complemented his speech a few months earlier about Russia creating an Iron Curtain that divided Europe. Churchill described a united Europe as based on France and Germany, offering a European perspective in the United Nations to complement the global perspective of the United Kingdom and the United

States. As a first step towards European unity, he recommended the creation of a Council of Europe. The Council was set up as an inter-governmental body to maintain standards approved by its forty-six member states. It was not intended to be a federal union. Nor did it have the power to carry out effective policies that would ensure economic, military or political security.

The approach that attracted the support of national governments was to build European institutions piecemeal by creating a trio of institutions that dealt with economic, military and political security. As long as the same governments were in all three institutions, they could co-ordinate their multiple priorities at home and in inter-governmental councils. French politicians took the lead in promoting this trio, so that Germany would be locked into institutions of interdependence before it regained the strength to pursue its national interests at the expense of its neighbours.

The leaders of national governments were predisposed to support the creation of supra-national institutions that might provide security. Many were cosmopolitan Europeans, having been born before 1914, when the boundaries of states were not defined by ethnicity and had their citizenship changed at least once by *force majeure*. They had lived through two wars that had imposed heavy costs in human life, in money and in political institutions. Their political ideology, whether socialist, Catholic or liberal, united them with politicians in other countries, while dividing them from fellow citizens with whom they competed for national office. The acceptance of inter-governmental institutions to achieve security did not make cosmopolitan politicians ignore their national interests. For many, engaging with interdependence through European institutions was a means to the end of national security.

The next section shows how the aspiration to unite Europe produced plans in the early 1950s for three complementary communities, but the defence and political communities failed to gain the endorsement of national parliaments. The second section shows how common interests led to the establishment of the European Economic Community (EEC) to create a common market that would be a cornerstone for European integration. While the EEC's powers and achievements were initially limited, the third section shows how the Community has expanded its economic powers and institutions through spillovers from existing policies and adding powers when crises occurred.

Securing control of coal and steel

The fear of German rearmament was common throughout Europe, including Germany. The first German chancellor, Konrad Adenauer, a Catholic former mayor of Cologne, had more sympathy for his French neighbours than for Prussian rulers and their Nazi successors. Although the German economy was in ruins in 1945, Allied forces could see that, as the German *Wiederaufbau* (rebuilding the ruins) progressed, it would again become a major power in Europe (John W. Young, 1990). The French government had the most fear, having lost three wars to Germany since 1870.

The development of the Cold War encouraged the revival of German industry to fuel the economic recovery of the whole of Western Europe. However, this also raised concerns about the need to control industries that could supply Germany with materials of war. In April 1949, the French government secured the agreement of occupying powers to an International Ruhr Authority vesting long-term control of the heartland of German industry in a consortium of France, Britain, the United States and the Benelux countries (Yoder, 1955). The French idea of strictly limiting German production of coal and steel was consistent with the view of the Prussian chancellor, Otto von Bismarck, who declared in 1862 that 'the great questions of the day will be decided by blood and iron [*Blut und Eisen*]'. However, the French position was in conflict with the American view that greater German industrial output was desirable for Europe's economic recovery.

Securing European control of materials of war. Five years and a day after the end of the Second World War in Europe the French foreign minister, Robert Schuman, put forward a plan to create a supra-national European Coal and Steel Community (ECSC). In Schuman's words, this would result in 'any war between France and Germany becoming not only unthinkable but materially impossible'. This date has since become the European Union's equivalent of the American Fourth of July. However, instead of celebrating independence it celebrates interdependence, the creation of a major European institution with the power to limit the sovereignty of its member governments. For both Adenauer and Schuman, the peaceful surrender of a very limited amount of sovereignty was a major boon, as they had lived through their country losing sovereignty due to military defeat. For the same reason, participation in the

ECSC was rejected by the British Labour government, which was nationalizing ownership of the British coal and steel industries.

German industrialists sought to protect their concentrated ownership of the coal and steel industries, but the American occupation authority insisted on breaking up trusts to avoid the ECSC becoming an exploitative cartel. For different reasons, the Schuman Plan was opposed both by the German Social Democrats and by supporters of Charles de Gaulle. Nonetheless, the ECSC was established in April 1951, with six members: France, Germany, the Benelux countries and Italy. Its headquarters were in Luxembourg, and the International Ruhr Authority was dissolved.

The institutions of the six-country ECSC were carefully designed to ensure that member states could control each other. A High Authority was created with an Executive issuing decisions that the coal and steel industries had to put into effect. While the member states nominated the members of the Executive, they were not national representatives but pledged to act in the supra-national interest of the Authority as a whole. Jean Monnet was its first president. A supra-national Court of Justice was established to interpret and enforce the powers granted to the Authority. There were three separate multi-national bodies to scrutinize the work of the supra-national High Authority. The Special Council of Ministers was composed of representatives of national governments charged with co-ordinating ECSC policies at the national level. To keep the chair of the Council weak, the position rotated between members every three months. The Council could not make decisions outside its limited competence.

There was a Common Assembly composed of politicians described as 'representatives of the peoples'. In fact they were national MPs nominated by their national parliament. The Assembly was expected to scrutinize the activities of the High Authority. While it did not have lawmaking powers, it did have the power to dismiss the Authority's chief officials. In addition a Consultative Committee was created to represent interest groups. Membership was divided equally between producers, workers, consumers and others working in the sector. It could comment on the broader implications of coal and steel policy but its formal endorsement was not needed for the Authority to act.

Given American pressure for German rearmament to counter the force of the Soviet bloc, in October 1950 Prime Minister René Pleven of France proposed the creation of a European Defence Community. France, Germany and other states would commit dozens of army divisions and much of their air force to the Defence Community. It would thereby prevent the creation of an independent German army. Nor would it compete with NATO, since the European Defence Community force would be under NATO's Supreme Allied Commander for military operations. In 1952 the six heads of governments in the ECSC signed a European Defence Community treaty.

To augment the Coal and Steel and Defence Communities, the Common Assembly of the ECSC proposed in 1952 the creation of a European Political Community. It was meant to have powers to co-ordinate foreign affairs and monetary policy as well as significant economic power (Griffiths, 1994). A draft treaty was prepared that made provision for a popularly elected lower house, a senate composed of representatives of national parliaments and a supra-national executive accountable to the parliament.

Treaties creating European institutions normally require each national parliament to ratify a document signed by its head of government before they can come into effect. In August 1954 the French National Assembly intensively debated whether to approve participation in a European Defence Community with a re-armed Germany. It rejected doing so by a vote of 319 to 264. This veto torpedoed the creation of a European Political Community but it did not stop the rearmament of Germany. The following year the Federal Republic was admitted to NATO, and control of European defence was outsourced to the United States.

In retrospect the ECSC can be seen as a forerunner of the European Economic Community and, at one remove, of the European Union. This was not an accident, but the intention of its protagonists. In putting forward the plan for a coal and steel institution, Robert Schuman described it as 'the first concrete step towards a European federation, imperative for the preservation of peace'.

Securing economic interests in a common market

The failure to institutionalize a trio of European institutions all at once did not discourage the ECSC governments from pursuing joint actions to further their security. For Belgium, Luxembourg and the Netherlands there was an added incentive: each lacked the resources to defend themselves in a clash with a bigger neighbour. For the French government, the memory of recent European wars inspired a goal of creating institutions that could prevent another war with Germany. For the German government the motive was to gain acceptance as a partner rather than a defeated aggressor.

From a political economy perspective, there were multiple reasons for seeking security through economic co-operation. The rise of extremist parties in Europe and the weakening of democratic institutions were often seen as the result of economic depression between the two world wars. While extremist right-wing parties were not a threat, communist parties looking to Moscow for security were major parties in both France and Italy, and the Federal Republic was competing with East Germany for the leadership of the German people.

The success of the European Coal and Steel Community encouraged its national leaders to seek further economic co-operation. Benelux ministers presented proposals for a customs union not restricted to coal and steel at a June 1955 meeting at Messina, Italy. The participants endorsed the proposals and asked the Belgian foreign minister, Paul-Henri Spaak, to draw up a detailed plan. The following year the Spaak Report recommended creating an economic institution that would reduce trade barriers and an institution to pool members' resources to develop atomic energy.

The EEC: More than a talking shop. The 1957 Treaty of Rome authorized the creation of a European Economic Community (EEC). The preamble of the treaty stated its aim was 'to lay the foundations of an ever-closer union among the peoples of Europe'. Its actual powers were much more limited than enthusiasts for European unity sought, because national governments, especially the French, did not want to accept substantial supra-national constraints. For the same reason the UK rejected membership (Hugo Young, 1998). The EEC was authorized to undertake measures promoting the free movement of goods, services and persons and to adopt a Common Agricultural Policy (CAP). In both cases a common market for the six member states had common external tariffs, thereby providing a degree of protection against foreign competition from low-cost countries as well as from the highly developed United States.

The EEC was established with a Commission of supra-national officials responsible for preparing policies within its competence. An inter-governmental Council of national ministers met quarterly to review

Community policies and discuss common problems. It was supported by national ambassadors posted in Brussels to monitor EEC activities. There was also a Parliamentary Assembly, consisting of members of national parliaments. The Court of the ECSC in Luxembourg became the Court of Justice of the European Communities.

Decisions in the Council were usually made by a consensus arrived at by negotiations in which a general agreement was reached without voting. France, Germany and Italy each had four votes; Belgium and the Netherlands two votes each; and Luxembourg one vote. If a vote was called on a Commission proposal, a qualified majority of twelve of the seventeen votes was required for approval. If a proposal was put forward by a member state, then at least four countries as well as twelve votes were required for approval. These rules meant that no large country had a veto on a decision and the three small countries relied on the Commission to avoid proposals that they would oppose. The need to negotiate slowed down the decision-making process.

The replacement of the pro-integration French Fourth Republic with a Fifth Republic headed by President Charles de Gaulle changed the position of France in European politics. De Gaulle favoured a *Europe des patries* in which national governments, especially those of big countries such as France, bargained to arrive at policies in their joint interest. De Gaulle was no federalist, but he welcomed the EEC as providing a shock stimulus to modernize the French economy and the CAP as absorbing part of the cost of subsidizing economically inefficient French peasants.

The Treaty of Rome called for the gradual creation of a customs union within twelve years in order to promote national economic growth and trade between member states. National economies that had invested to rebuild the damage of war were able to sustain growth after their recovery. Increasing prosperity generated acceptance of the EEC dismantling protectionist trade policies that countries had maintained before the Second World War. After prolonged bargaining, by 1968 the EEC had implemented the powers it was given to reduce trade barriers between member states.

Economic growth. The development of European institutions almost exactly coincided with what a French author called the *trente glorieuses*, thirty glorious years of sustained economic growth (Figure 3.1). It produced much more widespread prosperity than any European country had previously achieved

(Miotti and Sachwald, 2004). The starting point for what Germans called the *Wirtschaftswunder* (economic miracle) was rebuilding economic resources destroyed by war. From 1949 to 1954 the official gross national product of the Federal Republic grew by an annual average of 8.4 per cent (Rittershausen, 2007: 30).

The cumulative effect of three decades of economic growth was great, albeit not equal across Europe because of different national starting points. Annual growth of 6.1 per cent in the German economy quadrupled its size in a quarter-century. The modernization of the economies of France and Italy produced annual growth rates of almost 5 per cent, and their national economies trebled in the same period. While European institutions could claim to have contributed to economic growth, they were not the primary cause. Growth was greatest in Germany, where war had resulted in the creative destruction of much economic capacity and its replacement with up-to-date equipment.

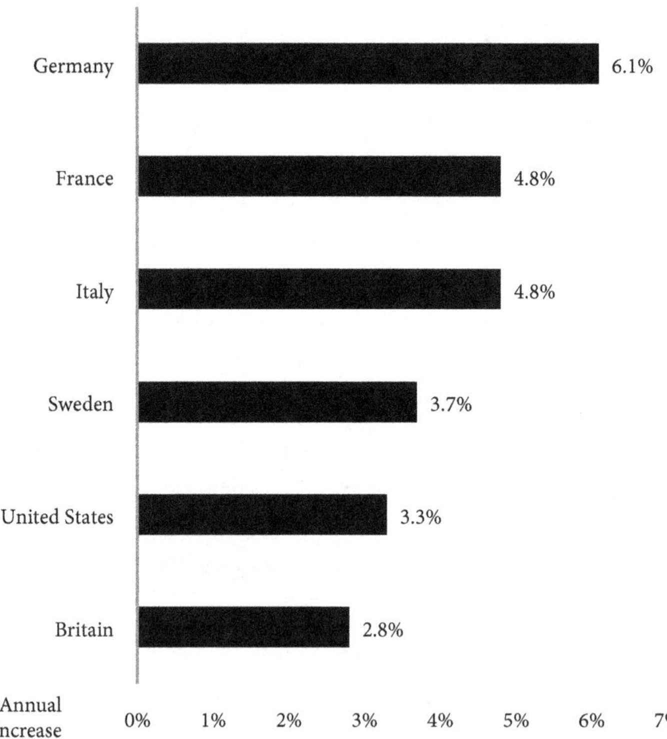

Figure 3.1 Average annual rate of GDP growth, 1950–76

Source: OECD statistics reported in Rose and Peters, 1978: Table A 2.1.

Growth was also higher in France and Italy because it was catching up by turning a heavily agricultural and regulated economy into a modern market economy. The United States, the United Kingdom and Sweden did not need to catch up because they had industrialized earlier and experienced growth rather than destruction during the war. While a correlation between growth and EEC membership was not proof of causation, advocates of European integration were ready to claim credit for it.

Building Europe through spillovers and crises

When the heads of government of the six founding EEC states met to discuss matters, they could easily sit around a family dinner table. This did not produce immediate agreement, but it did make it easier to bargain in ways that led to a positive outcome. While there were procedures to make decisions by a qualified majority vote, members preferred to reach decisions by consensus. Even if leaders of national governments did not get everything they wanted, they preferred to make compromises rather than become isolated by breaking the consensus. Thus, votes recording disagreements were the exception. The veto power was especially disliked by European federalists, since it made it easy for a single government to block measures enhancing the power of the EEC vis-à-vis member states. Nonetheless, heads of national governments favoured having it, as it was the ultimate guarantee that compromises would not include conditions against their vital political interests.

A major disagreement between France and the Commission on the funding of agricultural subsidies led to an 'empty chair' crisis in 1965. Under the Treaty of Rome, duties on agricultural and industrial products were due to be assigned to the Community, and the Commission wanted to use these to expand its resources. It also wanted an increase in majority voting without a veto. When the Commission's views appeared dominant, France recalled its representatives from Brussels and announced it would no longer participate in meetings of the EEC's Council. France was brought back to participation in the EEC by the Luxembourg Compromise. It stipulated that Council members would strive to adopt policies that respected the national interests of each member state. If a member state viewed a proposed policy as threatening its national interests, no decision would be taken until there was unanimous agreement. The immediate political effect was to induce caution in the Commission putting forward proposals.

By the mid-1970s European institutions appeared to be suffering 'a general malaise', preventing advancement towards the 'ever-closer union' promised by the Treaty of Rome (Dinan, 2010: 56). National governments complained that the European Commission was stifling progress through an excess of bureaucracy and a deficiency of imagination. The Council asked the Belgian Prime Minister Leo Tindemans, a committed federalist, to prepare a report defining what the term European Union meant. The Tindemans report (1976) set out a series of incremental changes to strengthen the EU. The report was put on the Council's agenda but no action was taken.

Small steps towards European integration were continuing through a process that Ernst Haas (1958) labelled 'spillovers', the feedback of unintended and sometimes unwanted consequences of earlier decisions. Policy could thereby become its own cause as pragmatic politicians and administrators sought to resolve functional problems by adding features to improve a policy rather than abandoning it (Wildavsky, 1979: 62–85). Haas argued that the momentum of expansion was immanent in the creation of the European Coal and Steel Community. To this incrementalist approach, Jean Monnet (1978: 304f) added the prospect of taking big steps towards greater political and economic integration when a crisis arises: 'People only accept change when they are faced with necessity and only recognise necessity when a crisis is upon them.' For example, the doubling in size of the EEC membership beginning in 1973 stimulated the development of institutions and the growing belief that political institutions ought to be democratic resulted in the European Parliament becoming directly elected in 1979 (see Section 5.2).

A new and partially committed member. While Britain has long been part of the European balance of military power, its prime ministers have had a world view shaped by an empire spread across continents. Engagement with the European continent has been intermittent. In 1945 the Attlee government's chief priorities were managing the peaceful transition from a British Empire to a Commonwealth and maintaining a special relationship with the United States. As a founder member of NATO, the UK gained not only military security but also a link with the American defence establishment.

When the British government was invited to participate in the formation of the ECSC and the European Economic Community, it remained aloof. It saw no advantage in integrating the British economy with Europe. This was the view of both the Labour government of Clement Attlee and of the Conservative government of Winston Churchill and Anthony Eden. In a speech to the 1962 Labour Party conference Hugh Gaitskell rejected giving up a thousand years of British (*sic*) history as an independent state to join a Janus-faced Europe that had produced Hitler and Mussolini as well as Goethe and Voltaire.

By 1961 British officials saw that the European institutions Britain had rejected were durable and growing in importance. Prime Minister Harold Macmillan sought British entry to the EEC in the hope that joining a larger and more dynamic economy would give the British economy a much-needed stimulus. Moreover, President John F. Kennedy's White House considered that British membership would be good for Anglo-American relations and offset the desire of France to keep the United States at arm's length from European affairs. Macmillan made clear that joining the EEC would be subject to securing conditions to protect trade with the Commonwealth, particularly in foodstuffs, which were cheaper than in Europe. He told Parliament that EEC membership would involve economic integration without political integration (Deighton and Ludlow, 1995).

The British application to join the EEC was vetoed by French President Charles de Gaulle in January 1963, using arguments that Brexiters were to use half a century later. De Gaulle described Britain as a nation differing profoundly from continental Europe. 'It is maritime; it is bound by trade, by its markets to the most diverse array of countries – and often the most far-flung, and its habits and traditions are very different' (France 24, 2019). De Gaulle also saw Britain's ties with Washington as a Trojan horse. If Britain joined the EEC it would 'become a colossal Atlantic community under American domination'. By vetoing Britain's application for membership, de Gaulle was also protecting the preeminence in the EEC of a Franco-German alliance.

As Britain's economic problems intensified and the pound fell in value, the Labour government of Harold Wilson put in a qualified application for EEC membership in 1967. Once again President de Gaulle vetoed the British application. Instead of pointing to differences in past traditions, he emphasized that Britain's weak sterling and importing cheap foodstuffs were incompatible with the economy that the EEC was building. If Britain wanted to join the EEC, de Gaulle claimed it would need 'a fundamental and radical transformation'.

When Edward Heath became prime minister in 1970, for the first and last time the UK had a prime minister with a commitment to securing peace and prosperity through building new European institutions. As a student he had seen a Nuremberg rally addressed by Hitler and as a soldier he fought to liberate France and was in the ruins of Hamburg on V-E Day. De Gaulle's resignation as president of France in 1969 unlocked the door to Britain joining the EEC, and the Heath government promptly put forward Britain's third application.

Heath's commitment to Europe could not remove problems from previous applications, such as Britain's reliance on cheap Commonwealth foodstuffs, but Heath did have the political drive to find a way to resolve difficulties. Moreover, political conditions had changed on the continent. The new French president, Georges Pompidou, welcomed British entry. Among other reasons, it would provide a potential ally since Germany, with Willy Brandt as chancellor, was pursuing an *Ostpolitik* that gave priority to German re-unification. When the critical House of Commons vote endorsing EU membership was held on 28 October 1971, both parties were divided. British entry carried by 356 votes to 244; the 69 Labour MPs defying their party line to vote for EU entry offset the 39 Conservative MPs voting against EU membership. In 1973 the UK became a member of the European Economic Community.

On becoming prime minister again in 1974, Harold Wilson sought to renegotiate the terms of British membership as a means of holding together a Labour Party divided on Europe. Wilson also pledged to hold a referendum on the results of the renegotiation about Britain's budgetary contribution, the Common Agricultural Policy and Britain's trade with Commonwealth countries. After protracted haggling that undermined a significant portion of the goodwill that Heath had gained, Wilson pronounced the terms satisfactory. Roy Jenkins, then a Labour MP and subsequently president of the European Commission, described the renegotiation as producing 'the minimum of results with the maximum ill-will' (1991: 375; George, 1998).

The referendum question the British electorate was asked to decide in 1975 was: *Do you think that the United Kingdom should stay in the European Community (the Common Market)?* The reference to the Common Market reflected the British view that the EEC was simply an institution offering a larger market for British exports. Margaret Thatcher, who had replaced Heath as leader of the Conservative Party, campaigned for a yes vote, arguing, 'To take a gamble of leaving Europe would be reckless in the extreme.' Opponents such as Enoch Powell and Tony Benn described the EEC in political terms as a threat to the sovereignty of the British Parliament. The 1975 referendum produced a 67.2 per cent vote in favour of membership with an absolute majority in favour in all four nations of the UK (Butler and Kitzinger, 1976). In the words of British diplomat Stephen Wall (2020), 'Britons were reluctant Europeans.'

A crisis of economic growth. In 1975 a global recession ended the thirty glorious years of economic growth. Instead of expanding, the gross domestic product of major European countries shrank. There was a contraction of as much as 3.7 per cent in the Italian economy and 3.2 per cent in Germany. National governments were under pressure to respond, since the Common Market's trade powers were inadequate to provide a prompt and effective remedy. Unexpected stagflation (low growth and high inflation) created a crisis in economic theory too. Prevailing Keynesian theories of stimulating demand and corporatist regulations to promote economic growth were in conflict with Milton Friedman's priority of managing the money supply and deregulating the economy (Rose and Peters, 1978).

The crisis in national economies created an opportunity for the European Economic Community to expand its powers. Major fluctuations in the exchange rates of currencies of member states threatened cross-national trade within the Common Market. To deal with this problem, the Commission president Roy Jenkins proposed 'a great leap forward', the creation of a European Monetary System (EMS). This gained the support of the German chancellor Helmut Schmidt, and François Mitterrand, the French president, as it fitted with their national priorities. It also met with the usual scepticism of a British prime minister, Labour leader Jim Callaghan. As a result, participation was voluntary in the EMS. It created a European Currency Unit (ECU) as a weighted average of the currencies of the participating states and an Exchange Rate Mechanism that let national currencies fluctuate within fixed margins, thereby limiting volatility and maintaining the liquidity needed for Common Market trade. This lasted until 1999, when the spillovers it created led to its replacement by the Economic and Monetary Union (EMU).

The economic crisis also created a demand to get rid of many non-tariff restrictions on trade that were obstacles to achieving a Common Market in fact as well as name. A paper by British Prime Minister Margaret Thatcher to the EEC's 1985 Fontainebleau summit called for promoting economic growth through the creation of a 'genuine common market in goods and services which is envisaged in the Treaty of Rome'. The Commission supported creating a single European market, giving it more powers to promote trade between member states and the free movement of goods, people, services and capital.

Whereas Thatcher saw a single European market as an end in itself, Jacques Delors, the president of the European Commission and a committed federalist, viewed it as likely to have spillovers furthering both political and economic integration (see Chapter 5). This led to the 1986 Single European Act that introduced changes in the legislative process and expanded the use of a qualified majority to make it easier to adopt legislation. The treaty also declared that member states sought 'to transform relations as a whole among their States into a European Union'.

Membership grows. The first round of enlargement began with four countries – the UK, Denmark, Ireland and Norway – applying for EEC membership. All four countries were granted membership contingent on ratification by their national parliament. Because of constitutional obligations or domestic political calculations, each government called a referendum asking its voters to endorse membership (Mendez, Mendez and Triga, 2014). Instead of a consensus, each referendum showed that voters were divided. The positive vote varied from five-sixths endorsing joining in Ireland, and about two-thirds in the UK and Denmark. The result in Norway showed that national divisions about EU membership could sometimes produce a majority against; 53.5 per cent of Norwegians rejected EEC membership.

The fall of Mediterranean dictatorships in Greece, Spain and Portugal led each new government to apply for admission to the EEC. All three saw it as a means of strengthening their democratic institutions. While accepting their political motives, existing EEC members were concerned about the economic consequences of admission. All three countries had large agricultural labour forces and levels of income qualifying them for substantial grants from the EEC's budget that would have to come from existing member states. However, there was a common political desire to support the spread of democracy in

Europe and political considerations overcame economic self-interest. The EEC admitted Greece after six years of evaluation and Spain and Portugal after nine years.

The enlargement of the EEC necessarily involved the revision of Council voting rules. The principle was maintained of requiring a qualified majority to ensure Council approval. The UK received ten votes, the same as three other populous member states, and Denmark and Ireland each received three votes. This meant that if the UK disapproved, a policy could carry with the support of three big states plus three or more of the smaller states. When Greece joined, it received five votes as did Portugal, and Spain received eight votes. The net effect of increasing EEC membership was to boost the collective importance of less populous states.

By the 1980s efforts to achieve European security by building European institutions had achieved one hit and one big miss. As the founders of the European Coal and Steel Community had intended, it led to the creation of a single European market and strengthened protection against global markets. The sturdiness of these foundations has been demonstrated by the subsequent development of the European Union (see Chapter 5). Concurrently, the failure to achieve a European Defence Community in 1954 has meant that today the military security of Europe is not secured through a European institution but depends on decisions taken by the US government.

Bibliography

Butler, David and Kitzinger, Uwe, 1976. *The 1975 Referendum*. London: Macmillan.

Deighton, Anne and Ludlow, Piers, 1995. 'A Conditional Application: British Management of the First Attempt to Seek Membership of the EEC, 1961–3'. In Anne Deighton, ed., *Building Postwar Europe*, London: Palgrave Macmillan, 107–26.

Dinan, Desmond, 2010. *Ever Closer Union*. London: Palgrave Macmillan, 4th edition.

France 24, 2019. 'Did Charles de Gaulle Foresee Brexit?'. www.france24.com/en/20191013-did-charles-de-gaulle-foresee-brexit. Accessed 20 August 2023.

George, Stephen, 1998. *An Awkward Partner: Britain in the European Community*. Oxford: Oxford University Press, 3rd edition.

Griffiths, Richard, 1994. 'Europe's First Constitution: The European Political Community, 1952–1954'. In Stephen Martin, ed., *The Construction of Europe*, Dordrecht: Springer, 19–39.

Haas, Ernst B., 1958. *The Uniting of Europe*. Stanford: Stanford University Press.

Jenkins, Roy, 1991. *Life at the Centre*. London: Macmillan.

Mayne, Richard J., Pinder, John and Roberts, John, 1990. *Federal Union: The Pioneers*. London: Palgrave Macmillan.

Mendez, Fernando, Mendez, Mario and Triga, Vasiliki, 2014. *Referendums and the European Union*. Cambridge: Cambridge University Press.

Miotti, Luis and Sachwald, Frédérique, 2004. *La croissance française 1950–2030. Le défi de l'innovation*. Paris: Ifri/La Documentation française.

Monnet, Jean, 1978. *Memoirs*. Garden City, NY: Doubleday.

Rittershausen, Johannes R. B., 2007. *The Postwar West German Economic Transition*. Cologne: University zu Koln, Institut fur Wirtschaftspolitik IWOP Discussion Paper 2007/1.

Rose, Richard and Peters, Guy, 1978. *Can Government Go Bankrupt?* New York: Basic Books.

Tindemans, Leo, 1976. *Report by Mr Leo Tindemans to the European Council*. Brussels: Bulletin of the European Communities Supplement 1/76.

Wall, Stephen, 2020. *Reluctant Europeans: Britain and the European Union from 1945 to Brexit*. Oxford: Oxford University Press.

Wildavsky, Aaron, 1979. *The Art and Craft of Policy Analysis*. London: Macmillan.

Yoder, Amos, 1955. 'The Ruhr Authority and the German Problem'. *Review of Politics*, 17, 3, 345–58.

Young, Hugo, 1998. *This Blessed Plot: Britain and Europe from Churchill to Blair*. London: Macmillan.

Young, John W., 1990. *France, the Cold War and the Western Alliance, 1944–1949*. New York: St Martin's Press.

Part Two

Security boundaries change

4

Perestroika restructures Europe

There has always been an ambivalence about whether Russia was part of Europe. By the seventeenth century the Russian tsar's territory had extended eastwards to Siberia and the borders of China; its westward exposure was Byzantine, a claim to be a third Rome as head of the Eastern Orthodox Church. Peter the Great took major steps to integrate Russia with Europe, moving the capital from inland and eastward-looking Moscow to the new Baltic city of St Petersburg. The accession to power in 1762 of Catherine the Great, a German-born princess, strengthened European ties, as she was interested in the Enlightenment and French customs and language spread among the aristocracy. In the nineteenth century the empire expanded east towards Alaska and Japan and westwards to take in Finland and much of Poland. Equally important, from the Napoleonic wars to the First World War, other European states saw it as part of the European balance of power.

Communists in tsarist Russia saw themselves as part of a European movement in which Germany was central, as Marxists believed that the collapse of capitalism would start there as a consequence of its internal contradictions. To escape the tsarist police, Vladimir Lenin fled to London, while Leon Trotsky, who was educated in German in Odesa, settled in Vienna. European ties broke when some European governments, including Britain, gave military aid to anti-communist troops fighting the Bolshevik seizure of power in 1917. The failure of communists to take power in Germany and Hungary in the aftermath of the First World War turned the new regime inwards. Once in power after Lenin's death, Joseph Stalin promoted the policy of Socialism in One Country.

Both democratic and undemocratic governments in Europe shared distrust of the new Soviet Union. Adolf Hitler courted West European sympathies by suppressing German communists and using anti-communist rhetoric. Stalin took advantage of Hitler's offer to share in the conquest of Poland and the Baltic states in 1939. After Nazi Germany invaded the Soviet Union in June 1941, the latter turned into an ally of Britain and the United States.

The Second World War resulted in the return of Russia to Europe, but Soviet motives were different from those of Peter the Great. The aim was to gain territory not knowledge. The advance of Soviet troops into Berlin, Vienna and Prague made Stalin's government a European presence. Soviet military power, augmented by satellite communist regimes, made the USSR the biggest European military power until the creation of NATO extended the western boundary of Europe to the Potomac. Moscow adopted this definition of Europe by denouncing NATO members as American lackeys. Possession of atomic weapons confirmed the Soviet Union's status as a great power, with allies extending across continents from China to Ethiopia to Cuba. However, this did not make the Soviet Union a European country in the sense in which democratic governments use that term.

The Cold War drew a dividing line through Europe as it had existed before 1939. Moreover, it was stable until 1989. Neutral countries bordering the Soviet bloc such as Austria and Finland had economic links with it and produced goods and services that the command economies of the Soviet bloc could not manufacture (cf. Kornai, 1992). The American government did not support attempts to overthrow communist regimes. It sought to keep the Cold War stable by continuously upgrading military defence to deter Soviet forces, and the latter did the same.

The restructuring of Europe came from the east, not the west, a consequence of the general secretary of the Communist Party of the Soviet Union (CPSU), Mikhail Gorbachev, trying to reform the Soviet system. In six years from 1985, the impact of Gorbachev's reforms went far beyond his expectations. The Soviet Union collapsed after his policy of *glasnost* (openness) made it permissible for Russians to say what they thought in public, and his complementary policy of *perestroika* (restructuring) opened fissures in a highly centralized party-state. At the end of December 1991 the Soviet Union broke up, and Soviet bloc countries that had previously been an integral part of Europe were free to return to a changed Europe.

The surprisingly quick collapse of the Soviet Union is the focus of the next section. It is followed by a section about how East European countries wanted to return to Europe. However, having been communist-dominated for four decades, they were different from their Western neighbours as well as from what they had been before. This was most evident when Germans raised in the East German Democratic Republic became citizens of the Federal Republic of Germany after the fall of the Berlin Wall. As the third section shows, the return to Europe meant more than the removal of borders. It meant joining NATO to have military security protected by Washington and joining the European Union to have economic security supported by Brussels.

Bloodless collapse of the Soviet Union

Mikhail Gorbachev had been an active communist from youth, joining the Communist Party of the Soviet Union at the age of nineteen in 1950. After graduating from university, he worked as a party official in the provinces, gaining first-hand experience of how the system worked in practice as distinct from Marxist theory. When Nikita Khrushchev introduced destalinization, Gorbachev supported the policy. Gradually rising up the ranks, he became a member of the Central Committee of the CPSU in 1978 and two years later the youngest member of the Politburo. After three older party general secretaries died between 1982 and 1985, Gorbachev became the party's youngest-ever general secretary.

Challenges within the Soviet Union. The centralization of power in the CPSU was a force for integrating its multi-ethnic population and its fifteen republics, including Ukraine, Belarus and three Baltic states on Europe's borders, and republics bordering Iran and China. Afghanistan was a nominally independent state under Soviet protection, and Soviet troops went to war there in 1979 after an Islamic revolt. Gorbachev inherited this war and learned that the Soviet army was not up to defeating a guerrilla force in territory very different from the plains of Eastern Europe. Soviet troops were withdrawn from Afghanistan in 1989.

While statistics of the Soviet non-market economy do not provide satisfactory data, indicators of living conditions showed challenges to the economic security of the population. In European societies where economic growth improved living conditions, life expectancy was rising steadily. However, during Leonid Brezhnev's time as general secretary between 1964 and 1982, the life expectancy of males fell (Rose and Munro, 2002: Figure 3.2). Likewise, the chronic inefficiencies of the Soviet non-market agricultural system led to the import of grain from the United States and other countries to avoid the risk of starvation (Dovring, 1980).

To maintain the internal security of the state against the risk of economic collapse, in 1986 Gorbachev sought to restructure the state-controlled command economy. The state remained the owner of large enterprises, including massive collective farms. However, the role of the State Planning Committee, Gosplan, was reduced from setting production targets for enterprises to issuing indicative economic guidelines and targets. After producing goods needed for specific state projects, enterprises became free to produce goods in response to demand and to set prices that covered the cost of what they produced. State enterprises were allowed to manage their contracts and trade with foreign importers and exporters, exposing them to competition with market economies. These reforms were followed by allowing the creation of privately owned businesses.

To support economic restructuring Gorbachev encouraged opening up the closed conduct of public affairs. This was a radical break with the Soviet system under Stalin, in which Communist Party officials sought to control what citizens were allowed to know through censorship and to shape their thoughts through continuous agitation and propaganda. Openness lowered the Iron Curtain, permitting the flow of books, goods and people into the country from Europe. In addition, Soviet citizens were allowed to travel outside the communist bloc to see how capitalist economies actually worked, as Gorbachev and his advisers had done. A tortoise-like step to democracy was the introduction of multiple candidates for election to lower-level offices in the party.

The Cold War challenged. Gorbachev proposed a radical restructuring of European security, rejecting the Cold War division of the continent and declaring that his country was part of a Common European Home. In a speech in Prague in 1987 he stated, 'We are resolutely against the division of the continent into military blocs facing each other, against the accumulation of military arsenals in Europe, against everything that is the source of the threat of war.' Two years later in a speech to the Council of Europe Gorbachev declared that the Common European Home 'rules out the probability of an armed clash and the very possibility of the use of force or the threat of force'. He called for the replacement of military deterrence by a doctrine of military restraint.

Gorbachev's efforts to restructure the Soviet Union at home and abroad were cautiously welcomed by Western leaders. After meeting him in person, Margaret Thatcher declared, 'We can do business together'. Ronald Reagan initially sought to put pressure on the Soviet Union by launching a Strategic Defence Initiative, colloquially described as Star Wars. It aimed to give the United States strategic dominance by creating a costly and technologically advanced missile system that the Soviet Union could not compete with. A meeting with Gorbachev in 1985 prompted Reagan to start negotiations on the control of nuclear arms; by 1987 a landmark agreement was reached between the United States and the Soviet Union for the control of intermediate-range nuclear weapons.

The fall of the Berlin Wall in November 1989 put paid to Gorbachev's initial hope for the Soviet Union to remain leader of a large bloc of communist states in a Common European Home. It also made the re-unification of Germany an imperative priority for Helmut Kohl, the German chancellor, and the prospect of the extension of NATO forces into former Soviet bloc territories an urgent issue for Gorbachev. The upshot was an agreement on German re-unification with President George H. W. Bush's regime, leading Gorbachev to think that NATO would not expand eastwards (National Security Archive, 1990).

Concurrently, Gorbachev's domestic restructuring had undermined his security as leader of the Soviet Union. The introduction of competitive elections within the Communist Party gave ambitious party members an opportunity to gain office without being beholden to higher-ranking officials. If they chose to do so, they could seek votes by campaigning against Gorbachev's reforms on the grounds that they had gone too far or that they had not gone far enough. Boris Yeltsin chose the latter course. A year after Gorbachev named him as a candidate member of the Politburo, Yeltsin resigned and called for changes in the economy far beyond *perestroika*. In 1989 Yeltsin was elected to the Congress of People's Deputies of the Soviet Union and from there gained a seat on the Supreme Soviet of the Soviet Union. In 1990 Yeltsin was elected to the Russian Congress and became chair of the Russian Soviet Federative Socialist Republic. The following year he won popular election as president of the Russian Republic with more than three times the vote of Gorbachev's candidate.

As evidence increased of the withering of the authority of the party-state, high-ranking communists saw Gorbachev as a threat to the security of the Soviet Union, the CPSU and their own careers. In August 1991 senior military and party officials attempted a *coup d'état*, arresting Gorbachev at his holiday estate, and stating that because of his 'illness' an emergency committee of senior communists would govern the Soviet Union. Acting as president of Russia, Boris Yeltsin repudiated their claim to power. Within four days the coup had collapsed and so had Gorbachev's political authority, which passed to Boris Yeltsin. As president of Russia, he organized leaders of Soviet republics to defend their position against being undermined by the central power of the Soviet party-state. By December 1991 the Soviet state was gone and the Cold War had ended, as there was no longer a Soviet armed force for NATO to contain.

Old lands return to Europe but not as before

The states freed to follow their own way by the Soviet collapse had no common origin. In the past they had variously been parts of the German Empire, the Habsburg Empire, the Ottoman Empire or the tsarist Russian Empire. Between the First and Second World Wars, each had been an independent undemocratic state with the exception of democratic Czechoslovakia. Being part of the Soviet bloc imposed a veneer of commonality on their political institutions and economies. As long as a regime was backed by Soviet force, there was a willingness to go along with the powers that be. As a Hungarian saying put it, 'We pretend to be communists and they pretend to believe us.'

Mikhail Gorbachev's restructuring of the Soviet Union was watched with great interest throughout the Soviet bloc. Communist rulers did not want to put their own security at risk by doing the same. However as *glasnost* unfolded in the Soviet Union, it gave licence to demands for fundamental change in Estonia, Latvia and Lithuania, three Baltic states that had been forcibly incorporated as republics of the Soviet Union at the end of the Second World War. Hungary stopped fortifying its border with Austria in spring 1989, and thousands of East Germans travelled there as a means of getting to West Germany. When the East German leader Erich Honecker called on Budapest and Moscow to show 'socialist unity' by closing this escape hatch from his regime, nothing was done.

East German Lutheran ministers began organizing prayers for peace, nominally consistent with Soviet policy but with a subtext meaning that peace would come from the relaxation of communist rule. Massive and peaceful street demonstrations demanding structural changes in the East German regime began in September 1989. The following month a speech by the Soviet foreign minister stated that the Soviet Union now recognized the freedom of Warsaw Pact countries to make their own choices about how to restructure their regime. This became known as the Sinatra Doctrine. When an official spokesperson asked if this could mean turning communist parties out of office, he referred to Frank Sinatra's song, 'I Did It My Way'. In November 1989 the East German government gave in to demonstrators and opened up the gates of the Berlin Wall. The break-up of the Soviet bloc of countries was complete before the Soviet Union itself fell apart.

Multiple transformations. The disintegration of the Soviet bloc triggered a series of transformations across Europe. The continent was no longer divided into two parts by an Iron Curtain. Instead, it was a common home to countries that had constituted Europe between the two world wars. Yet ex-communist countries were not the same as before. Following the fall of the Berlin Wall they had to undergo another transformation to again fit into the Europe that they had left.

Free elections were called promptly in order to confirm the repudiation of communist regimes by the mass of citizens. In countries such as Hungary and Poland, many senior communists showed their inherent opportunism by participating in the formation of social democratic parties that returned to office as part of an anti-communist coalition government. The parties that fought as defenders of communist institutions and practices received derisory votes.

Most ex-communist countries had little or no previous experience of free and fair elections, and the purging of civil society institutions meant that parties could not be organized by established interests. Moreover, the communist disrespect for the rule of law meant that democracy was being introduced backwards, before major pre-conditions existed making democracy secure (Rose and Shin, 2001). Nonetheless, all of the regimes created then have continued in place for a third of a century. Even Czechoslovakia, which broke into the Czech and Slovak republics, did so peacefully and maintained democratic institutions. Election victories since then of the Law and Justice Party in Poland and the Fidesz Party of Viktor Orbán in Hungary show that free elections could be won by a party that gave voice to nationalist traditions rather than liberal democratic values.

New regimes acted promptly to reduce the power of the state by privatizing major industries in which communists were embedded. Many of these privatized enterprises could only survive in a market economy by implementing major reductions in employment and real wages. Many liberal democratic economists adopted a quasi-Marxist view that the immediate insecurity generated by the transition to a market economy would result in the return of authoritarian regimes. They forgot that people saw freedom from communist control of their daily lives as priceless, and decades of living with shortages of consumer goods in a non-market economy had made people patient (Rose, 1997).

Restructuring European security

The founders of European institutions were well aware that Europe has no fixed boundaries: they had seen its boundaries change more than once in their lifetime. Thus, conditions for EU membership have always avoided reference to geographical boundaries and there has always been a readiness to welcome more members. Before the Soviet Union collapsed, the EEC had twelve members with boundaries extending from the Eastern Mediterranean to the Atlantic coast of Ireland. Since the collapse of the Soviet Union the EU has more than doubled in size to twenty-seven members, and a willingness to discuss membership with Turkey and Iceland shows that its boundaries can extend even further east and west. However, the guarantor of European military security is not in Europe but in the United States. NATO was founded with twelve members in 1949. Since the fall of the Berlin Wall it has grown to thirty-one states from the United States and Canada to Turkey.

When leaders of ex-communist states talked about the return to Europe, they had two Europes in mind. To gain military security, they wanted to become part of North Atlantic Europe by joining NATO. To gain economic and political security, they wanted to become members of the European Union. The addition of many member states did not restructure NATO: the United States remained its hegemon. However, the increase in the EU's size and diversity has created pressures for change in the European Union.

Enlarging NATO. The collapse of the Soviet Union replaced the clear and present threat of Soviet armed forces with a potential threat from a nuclear-armed Russian Federation. Drawing on their past experience, ex-communist countries had no doubt about what they wanted. While membership in NATO would not change the danger of being close to Russia, it would extend their security to the Potomac. Membership offered far greater deterrence to a potential Russian aggressor than any ex-communist state could produce on its own.

The United States' immediate priority was to ensure that the break-up of the Soviet Union did not lead to its stock of nuclear weapons passing into multiple hands. This was a priority of the new Russian state too. There was co-operation in securing the transfer of weapons to Moscow from three ex-republics, including Ukraine. The second priority was to secure the removal of Soviet troops from East Germany. The Russian government agreed this after receiving unwritten assurances that withdrawal of its troops need not lead to the eastward expansion of NATO. Once this had occurred, Washington was prepared to take advantage of the weakness of Russia to respond positively to the desire of ex-communist countries for NATO membership (Shifrinson, 2016). While this was resented by Russian officials at the time and even more by Vladimir Putin subsequently, the support that President Clinton's administration gave the Yeltsin presidency muted Russia's opposition.

By joining NATO, ex-communist countries switched from being subject to one military hegemon to another hegemon, the United States, which they trusted to use its military might to deter another Russian occupation. For the Pentagon, being able to have ground troops close to Russia's borders was a major gain and for Germany as well. Since military service had been compulsory in Soviet times, these new NATO members contributed trained anti-Soviet recruits understanding the strengths and weaknesses of Soviet forces in which they had once served. In 1999 the Czech Republic, Hungary and Poland joined NATO and six additional states – Estonia, Latvia, Lithuania, Bulgaria, Romania and Slovakia – joined in 2004. Austria did not, as remaining neutral was a condition of Soviet forces withdrawing from Vienna in 1955.

While the break-up of the Soviet bloc in Eastern Europe occurred peacefully, the restructuring of the multi-ethnic Republic of Yugoslavia was violent. After the end of the Second World War, Josip Tito had established a centralized state independent of Moscow. Not only was the state multi-ethnic but there were large ethnic minorities within its constituent republics. Opening up its politics in the 1980s allowed minority ethnic politicians to promote demands to loosen the power of the centralized state and rekindled ethnic enmities from a 1940s civil war. Free elections in 1990 entrenched ethnic divisions, and the following year military conflict broke out between Croatia and the Serbian-dominated Yugoslav army. By 1996 all six of Yugoslavia's republics had become independent states but not all had settled boundaries.

A major Balkan objective of neighbouring European states has been containment, the prevention of armed conflict within the former Yugoslavia spilling into their territory. Active diplomacy by the United States, neighbouring countries such as Austria and the EU has achieved this. Four of the successor states of Yugoslavia – Slovenia, Croatia, Montenegro and North Macedonia – have become members of NATO but not Serbia and Bosnia-Herzegovina. Since the conflict in the newly created Republic of Kosovo borders three NATO members, NATO has invoked a United Nations resolution to send a small military force to deter Serbian aggression and prevent conflict spreading.

In ex-communist countries the biggest potential ethnic challenge to security came from large minorities of Russians settled in Estonia and Latvia after the end of the Second World War. At that time the Baltic states were forcibly integrated into the Soviet Union, and Russian was made the official language. Russian immigrants were doubly advantaged: they tended to have better communist connections with Moscow and enjoyed a higher standard of living than in Russia. Both of these advantages were lost when Baltic majorities gained control of government and enacted laws restricting their citizenship. However, the economic and political conditions of Russia under President Boris Yeltsin put them off either turning to Moscow for support or instigating domestic violence. Instead, leaders of the Russian minorities sought help from the EU to gain fair terms for inclusion in the Baltic state in which they resided.

Enlarging the European Union. The proponents of European integration have always had the ambition of admitting more states so that the EU would include all countries within Europe, however the continent is defined. The political assumption is that bigger is better, since adding members increases the number of countries and the millions of people for whom the European Union can speak and act. However, broadening increases the difficulty of reaching collective decisions, since the interests of more countries have to be taken into account.

The difficulties of enlarging the EU escalate when adding more states creates losers as well as winners if the economies of new member states are below the average EU economy, causing the redistribution of EU cohesion funds from existing members to less well-off new members (cf. Berglof et al., 2008). For smaller states, gross differences in population are an attraction of EU membership since it gives them access to a market much larger than their own. Less prosperous states receive social cohesion funds intended to raise their economies to the level of the average EU member. Joining NATO gives smaller states the protection of American armed forces with a firepower of up to 100 times more than their own military.

There was no doubt that ex-communist countries belonged in Europe, since they had historically been part of a common European home. Many had been part of multi-national empires ruled from Vienna, Berlin or Stockholm. Nor was there any doubt that their citizens wanted to be integrated into Europe. A 1991 survey of public opinion in Czechoslovakia, Hungary and Poland asked what country they would like their country to emulate. An average of 35 per cent named Germany, 29 per cent Sweden and 14 per cent other European countries. Only 18 per cent named the United States, and less than 1 per cent chose the Soviet Union (Rose, 1996: Table 2.1).

Established European democracies had no desire to see neighbouring countries left in limbo on their borders (cf. Rehn, 2006; Schimmelfennig and Sedelmeier, 2005). However, accession to the European Union challenged both the applicants and the EU. The legacy of communism meant that the political and economic institutions of applicants did not conform to European standards. While competitive elections could be quickly introduced and observed, the procedures central to the workings of a Single Europe Market and a rule-of-law *Rechtsstaat* have taken much longer. There were fears in Western Europe that low wages would lead to a flight of jobs to Eastern Europe. There was also a hope that after joining the European Union standards of governance would rise. As Spaniards said when their country became a new democracy after the death of Franco, 'If Spain is the problem, Europe is the solution'.

At the 1993 Council of Ministers meeting in Copenhagen, the EU set out five criteria that the applicant countries should meet: having democratic institutions, the rule of law, respect for human rights, an effective public administration and a functioning market economy. Security issues were left to NATO. The requirement of a functioning market economy avoided specifying a particular type of market economy. Member states have differed between the social market economy of Germany, the French tradition of a mercantilist economy and the market economy of Thatcher's Britain. Copenhagen criteria avoided specifying any quantitative indicators of economic performance such as gross domestic product per capita.

In Communist planned economies, people got by juggling resources from three economies: the official economy, making money in the unofficial economy, and producing goods and services in their household without any money changing hands (Rose, 2009: Figure 6.1). While communist economies were able to raise living standards significantly, they were simultaneously falling behind neighbouring market economies. In default of a common money measure, automobile ownership provides an objective indicator of the widening gap in living standards between the two systems. In 1949 there was only a gap of seven cars per 1,000 people between East and West Germans, because almost 99 per cent of Germans were without a car. By 1970 car ownership had spread on both sides of the Berlin Wall but East Germany had started falling behind. There was a gap of 155 automobiles per 1,000 between the two parts of the divided Germany and it was wider still when the Berlin Wall fell (Rose, 2009: Figure 3.1).

Between the fall of the Berlin Wall and entry to the European Union, there was more than a decade for ex-communist countries to complete the transformation of a non-market economy to a market economy. In 2007 the restructuring of Europe was completed by the admission to the EU of Bulgaria and Romania. Membership in the EU has given lower income countries greater economic security. This is most evident in the receipt of grants from the EU's social cohesion fund; the grants are intended to reduce inequality by promoting faster economic development. Enterprises are free to take advantage of their lower wage costs to export products to more prosperous countries in the Single Europe Market. Today four countries that had had non-market economies are now members of the eurozone.

The withdrawal of the United Kingdom from the EU had a marginal effect on the territorial scope of Europe compared to its impact on Britain. With the exception of Switzerland, Norway and troubled Balkan states, the European Union now covers the whole of Europe geographically. However, in terms of security against military aggression, the European Union's member states continue to look across the Atlantic to Washington for their defence.

Increasing diversity of states. Even though the population of each European country has changed relatively little since the Treaty of Rome was signed in 1957, the population of the European Union has more than doubled to 450 million people. Of this increase, almost half is due to the addition of countries that were formerly in the Soviet bloc. Today the European Union has a population almost one-third greater than the United States. If it were a state, which it is not (see Chapter 5), the EU would be the world's third most populous state.

The economic diversity of the European Union is no longer as simple as that of the Coal and Steel Community's six member states. Among the six founder states, the gross domestic product per capita of Italy, when measured by the World Bank in purchasing power terms, is two-thirds that of Germany. Among the fifteen older members of the EU, the GDP per capita of Ireland is more than three times that of Greece and Portugal. The admission of ex-communist states has increased diversity substantially. While differences among newer member states are limited, the difference with older EU members is substantial. Six ex-communist countries have a lower GDP per capita than Greece and as little as one-eighth the GDP of Ireland.

Cultural diversity is evident in the increased number of official languages that have come with expansion. In the six founding European countries, two had Romance language (France and Italy) and two a Germanic language (Germany and the Netherlands), while Belgium and Luxembourg used both types. As membership increased to fifteen, the principal change was the addition of English as an official language and its use as a *lingua franca* for commercial and inter-governmental relations. With further expansion, more language families have been added, including Slavic, Finno-Ugric, Baltic and Arabic. The EU now translates official documents and laws into twenty-four official languages.

Political diversity has been increased by introducing a distinction between old and new democracies. Among founder members the rule of law and free elections began to be introduced in the late nineteenth century. By contrast, countries of Eastern Europe were governed by a variety of undemocratic regimes between the two world wars. All were subject to a communist regime that relied on an aggressive party apparatus to restrict individual freedom and governed on the basis that the Communist Party's ends justified its means. When applying for admission, each country could show evidence of democratic elections and reformed political institutions, but none had had the time to become an established democracy.

Different political histories are reflected today in the level of corruption in government. Corruption had been accepted in communist systems as a way of getting things done, while unacceptable in countries that had institutionalized governance by the rule of law before they became electoral democracies (cf. Rose and Shin, 2001). On the 100-point Transparency International's 2023 Corruption Perceptions Index, EU member states differed by as much as 48 points. Scandinavian countries had the highest Index scores, led by Denmark, 90. Five founder members had scores between 71 and 79, and four Mediterranean countries had scores lower than that. Ex-communist states showed a great deal of diversity, ranging from a Corruption Index of 76 for Estonia to 42 for Hungary.

Diversity has put pressure on the European Union's oft-repeated claim that its members share common values. Established systems are usually seen as liberal democracies. The adjective liberal adds to free elections the protection of individual and minority rights, parliamentary checks on executive authority and an independent judiciary enforcing the rule of law (see e.g. Diamond, 2008).

Governments of Hungary and Poland have challenged liberal democratic values. When diversity results in persisting clashes about European values and practices, the EU must accommodate them, since it has no power to expel states. Viktor Orbán, the prime minister of Hungary since 2014, cites Singapore and China as positive examples of his approach, illiberal democracy, and his populist Fidesz Party government has enacted illiberal laws that threaten the independence of the judiciary and the checks and balances that maintain the rule of law as a restraint government power (see, e.g. Scicluna and Auer, 2019; Lorenz and Anders, 2021). In return, Orbán has been charged by the EU with violating EU rules concerning the rights of asylum seekers and open-market rules of the Single Europe Market. The Polish Law and Justice Party promotes a national-conservative alternative to liberal democracy. While in government, it has placed the sovereignty of Poland above the authority of the European Union. The Civic Coalition government formed after the 2023 election is now trying to get rid of undemocratic measures of its predecessor.

Among the EU's member states there is substantial diversity in the extent to which national governments practise liberal democracy. The Liberal Democracy Index, which combines expert ratings of 71 indicators of democracy (V-Dem Institute, 2023: 48ff), shows that the restructuring of Europe has increased differences in democratic practice among member states. On V-Dem's 100-point Liberal Democracy Index there is now a range of 54 points between the highest-ranking countries, Denmark and Sweden, 88, and the lowest ranked, Hungary 34. There is a difference in liberal democratic governance of only five points between the six founder states of the European Union, but a range of 50 points between the new member states of Estonia and Hungary.

Enlarging the European Union to twenty-seven members has had a double effect. It increases the collective resources of the EU and simultaneously broadens the ways in which member states view their security. What happens at the EU level now has a greater economic impact on Europeans. However, getting a consensus about EU policies is more difficult since the interests of four times as many countries must be taken into account. In a smaller EU, members are likely to have more interests in common, whereas expanding the number of members increases the diversity of countries that a policy must accommodate. When a consensus cannot be reached, like-minded governments can join together in institutions for specific problem-solving purposes as an alternative to the diffuse goal of European integration (cf. De Vries, Leuffen and Schimmelfennig, 2023). Thus, while a majority of EU countries have adopted the euro, there are still eight different currencies in use among member states.

Bibliography

Berglof, Erik, Burkart, Mike, Friebel, Guido and Palseva, Elena, 2008. 'Widening and Deepening: Reforming the European Union'. *American Economic Review*, 98, 2, 133–7.

De Vries, Catherine F., Leuffen, Derik and Schimmelfennig, Frank, eds., 2023. 'Differentiated Integration in the European Union'. *European Union Politics* (special issue), 24, 1, 3–235.

Diamond, Larry, 2008. *The Spirit of Democracy*. New York: Times Books.

Dovring, Folke. 'Soviet Agriculture in 1980'. *Current History*, 79, 459, 88–106.

Kornai, Janos, 1992. *The Socialist System: The Political Economy of Communism*. Princeton: Princeton University Press.

Lorenz, Astrid and Anders, Lisa H., eds., 2021. *Illiberal Trends and Anti-EU Politics in East Central Europe*. London: Palgrave Macmillan.

National Security Archive, 1990. https://nsarchive.gwu.edu/document/16135-document-21-record-conversation-between. Accessed 3 September 2023.

Rehn, Olli, 2006. *Europe's Next Frontiers*. Baden-Baden: Nomos.

Rose, Richard, 1996. *What Is Europe?* London: HarperCollins.

Rose, Richard, 1997. 'How Patient Are People in Post-Communist Societies?'. *World Affairs*, 159, 3, 130–44.

Rose, Richard, 2009. *Understanding Post-Communist Transformation: A Bottom Up Approach*. London: Routledge.

Rose, Richard and Munro, Neil, 2002. *Elections without Order: Russia's Challenge to Vladimir Putin*. Cambridge: Cambridge University Press.

Rose, Richard and Shin, Doh Chull, 2001. 'Democratization Backwards: The Problem of Third-Wave Democracies'. *British Journal of Political Science*, 31, 2, 331–54.

Schimmelfennig, Frank and Sedelmeier, Ulrich, eds., 2005. *The Europeanization of Central and Eastern Europe*. Ithaca, NY: Cornell University Press.

Scicluna, Nicole and Auer, Stefan, 2019. 'Europe's Constitutional Unsettlement: Testing the Political Limits of Legal Integration'. *International Affairs*, 99, 2, 769–85.

Shifrinson, Joshua B. Itzkowitz, 2016. 'Deal or No Deal? The End of the Cold War and the US Offer to Limit NATO Expansion'. *International Security*, 40, 4, 7–44.

V-Dem Institute, 2023. *Democracy Report 2023: Defiance in the Face of Autocratization*. Gothenburg: University of Gothenburg.

5

A stronger union but not a state

The leaders of European institutions were clear about their goal: the integration of European countries in a union with powers of a state. They have been flexible, broadening the EU's membership and deepening its powers. Increasing the number of members does not reduce its powers. The *acquis communautaire* means that in order to gain EU membership an applicant country must accept all the policies that have previously been adopted. Thus, the only direction in which European integration can move is forwards.

Political agreement about short-term benefits is a critical condition for introducing policies that deepen the EU. Leaving long-term goals vague or unspecified can be helpful in reaching an agreement when governments disagree about long-term goals. For example, the first generation of national leaders differed in their idea of what sort of Europe they hoped to create. The goal of General Charles de Gaulle was a *Europe des patries*, in which national governments could co-operate in their national interests, and France would enhance its European influence. By contrast, the Belgian socialist Paul-Henri Spaak was a federalist who saw supra-national institutions as the best way to advance economic and military security. Ever-increasing political integration created so great a conflict with the British vision of Europe as simply a common market that it was finally resolved by Brexit.

Europe's leaders must be patient about the tempo at which European integration increases, because of complicated rules about making EU decisions. To adopt a new treaty that can deepen the EU's powers requires unanimous approval; broadening membership likewise requires unanimity. Making use of existing powers to strengthen policies requires negotiations that produce a consensus in which all members get most but not all of what they want (Thomson, 2012). If there is no consensus, additional powers can be adopted by a coalition of the willing, that is, states that see a policy as beneficial. Temporarily this results in differentiated integration. If non-adopters later join in a new policy, this creates a two-speed Europe of early and late adopters of integration policy. If they do not, the European Union becomes a multi-dimensional institution with variable geometry, in which the number of member states participating in major activities varies from policy to policy.

The EU's powers are greatest in economic security. The logic of the stream-of-commerce doctrine has been used by socialists such as Jacques Delors to achieve the extension of the EU's influence on policies affecting the labour market, social conditions and the environment. The Lisbon Treaty's Article 3 confirmed the EU's exclusive powers over trade in the internal market of member states and trade between EU countries and non-member states. The impact of the EU's power in dealing with non-member states has been particularly felt by the UK following its withdrawal from the European Union.

This chapter describes the different ways in which European institutions have been deepened and broadened to make the European political economy more secure in a global economy. It has then sought to make its political institutions more democratically legitimate by introducing the direct election of the European Parliament (EP). The chapter concludes by showing that strengthening institutions of the European Union does not make it a state, which requires a military force to defend its citizens.

Making Europe's political economy more secure

When the European Coal and Steel Community was founded in 1951, there was no such thing as a global economy, nor was there a European economy. European states had responded to industrialization by adopting laws to regulate national industries and often were the owners of key services such as electricity, transport and armaments. They also adopted regulations to protect national industries and their peasant economy from foreign competition. The ravages of the Second World War massively damaged national economies without leaving anything in their place.

The Treaty of Rome was a conscious effort to create a European political economy, as the six founding national governments agreed in principle to the dismantling of protectionist laws and to the European Economic Community encouraging more trade between member states. Three decades after the Treaty of Rome was signed, the Single European Act (see Section 3.3) gave the EEC more powers to dismantle national laws that were obstructing a European economy and to promote four economic freedoms: the free movement of goods, services, people and capital in a market of hundreds of millions of people.

Concurrently, a global economy was being created by an increase in global trade in goods and services and economic growth in populous countries outside Europe. In 1960, three of the continent's largest economies, West Germany, the UK and France, were among the world's five largest economies. Up to a point the creation of the Single European Market increased the weight of the European economy. In gross domestic product it has become equal to the United States.

The high growth rates and massive population of a number of developing countries have challenged the global importance of the European economy. By 2010 the GDP of China had overtaken the GDP of each of Europe's four largest national economies. While the single market greatly increased trade between countries within Europe, the economic growth of China, Japan and the Republic of Korea involved a high level of exports to other continents.

Building a mountain of euros. Trade within the single market initially involved payment in twelve different national currencies and the exchange rate of the Deutsche Mark, French franc, Italian lira and other national currencies fluctuated daily. The rates were not set by a European institution but by the so-called gnomes of Zurich, the Swiss bankers that dominated the speculative market for the exchange of European currencies. Businesses that traded outside the single market could use a thirteenth currency, the US dollar, with its daily value influenced by what happened in Wall Street and Washington.

The fragmentation of currencies within the European political economy was recognized as a major handicap by advocates of European integration as well as by many professional economists. The economic theory supporting the creation of the eurozone was that replacing the many national currencies with a single multi-national euro would benefit all eurozone countries. The political theory supporting the eurozone was that it would be an irrevocable step towards European integration.

The European Monetary System had already introduced the European Currency Unit (ECU) to provide a common accounting unit for use in cross-national economic analysis rather than what international financial institutions used, the American dollar. The ECU reflected the value of an artificial basket of currencies of member states, weighted according to the share of the country in the EU's total output. It was thus substantially influenced by the size of the West German economy and even more by the economy of a unified Germany. In a 1988 report, Jacques Delors recommended the creation of a European Monetary Union in order to reduce currency fluctuations and begin the process of creating a single European currency.

The 1992 Maastricht Treaty created the European Central Bank (ECB) to control the euro and supervise national economic policies. Its headquarters was placed in Frankfurt am Main to distance it from the EU headquarters in Brussels. The ECB's technocratic directors were experts in monetary policy rather than representatives of national governments. While the German Bundesbank lost the right to issue the Deutsche Mark, its ideology was dominant in the Stability and Growth Pact adopted in 1997. The pact gave priority to keeping inflation low by limiting the spending of national governments. This reflected the triumph of the monetarist theory of Milton Friedman of the University of Chicago over the readiness of Keynesian economists to finance economic growth through deficit financing.

The fragmentation of the Single European Market into more than a dozen currencies was reduced by the introduction of the euro as a common currency of twelve countries that became members of the eurozone in 2002. Jacques Delors could no longer spend French francs, but he gained something priceless, a major step forward in European integration. There was disagreement among EU members about joining the eurozone (see Artis and Rose, 2002). Sweden is not a member because it would mean giving up its strategy of using monetary policy to minimize unemployment rather than inflation. Denmark was not a member because a national referendum rejected adopting the euro. The UK was not a member because Gordon Brown, then head of the British Treasury, had no wish to surrender any of its economic powers to the European Central Bank. Five non-members are East European countries formally committed to become eurozone members by the terms of their admission to the EU. None has yet shown the political will and economic strength to justify eurozone admission.

The capacity of the eurozone to promote economic security was first tested by sovereign debt crises beginning in 2009 in four Mediterranean countries plus Ireland. They had taken advantage of being able to borrow money at the low eurozone interest rates, and North European financial institutions were ready to make loans denominated in a stable currency, the euro. These borrowings created large debts that national governments could not refinance by devaluation, since they no longer had a national currency. They could only get out of their financial black hole with assistance from the European Central Bank. The ECB created financial stabilization programmes and loans offering unlimited support to governments participating in its bailout programmes, which imposed significant cuts in public spending. This was subsequently described by ECB President Mario Draghi as a policy of 'We will do what it takes.' National finances stabilized as monetarist theory predicted, while economic growth dropped, as Keynesian theory predicted.

The final test of the internal strength of the eurozone came in 2015, when the left-wing Syriza government of Greece appeared to be considering leaving the eurozone and restoring its national currency. The approach was supported by some voices in Germany, which wanted rid of a eurozone member that had persistently violated eurozone rules. When the crunch came, the Syriza government abandoned the risky consequences of withdrawal and accepted remaining in the ECB. This confirmed the irrevocable nature of eurozone membership.

The economic and political effects of joining the eurozone have been mixed, involving trade-offs between reducing inflation and promoting economic growth. Notwithstanding this, by 2023 a total of twenty of the twenty-seven EU states were members of the eurozone, and additional states and territories were linking their currencies to the euro rather than the dollar. The much reduced fragmentation of national currencies has increased the influence of European institutions in global markets, as the ECB now speaks for a single currency used by 344 million people.

Making the European Union more legitimate

To get citizens to go along with the costs as well as benefits of decisions about economic and military security, European governments require legitimacy;

otherwise, people may not comply with policies that have visible and immediate costs. Legitimacy requires losers' consent, that is, people who vote for the losing party or against a particular law accepting that they are bound by the outcome (Anderson et al., 2005). Democratic elections also give losers the chance to reverse a government decision if they become winners at the next election.

The founders of European institutions accepted the importance of national elections, since they held office because they were election winners nationally. Moreover, when reviewing proposals for EU policies, they were prepared to argue for making changes on the grounds that otherwise a proposed measure would lose them votes. As long as changes would not be politically costly to other national leaders, their wishes could be accommodated. Leaders also belonged to a generation that believed political elites were well qualified to make foreign policies in the national interest without guidance from a mass electorate. Their views were in keeping with Aaron Wildavsky's (1975) theory of the two presidencies. While national parliaments were appropriate for debating domestic issues, in foreign policy no debate was necessary because the government represented the national interest.

Legitimacy is a particular problem for the European Union. It can claim legitimacy in international law because its existence and powers are set out in international treaties signed by the head of government of each member state. The treaties serve as a kind of constitution. The Court of Justice of the European Union has the authority to enforce its interpretation of the treaties on other EU institutions and on national governments. The European Commission, staffed by supra-national civil servants and headed by appointees of national governments, prepares laws and regulations subject to direction by the European Council and its associated Council of Ministers, which consists of senior ministers of national governments. As long as EU policies are in keeping with the powers and procedures set out in the treaties, its actions are legitimate in the sense of being consistent with international law.

The challenge of electoral legitimacy. Legal legitimacy is insufficient to confer democratic legitimacy on the European Union, since democratic legitimacy requires citizens giving their consent to government at the ballot box. The elected heads of national governments inherit the obligation to accept EU treaties from their long gone predecessors. Unlike a new national government, they cannot repeal EU commitments accepted by their predecessors because of the principle of the *acquis communautaire*. Thus, when British Prime Minister David Cameron, acting on his national election mandate, sought to renegotiate Britain's conditions of EU membership to reduce the influence of Brussels on the UK, the EU refused to do so. The dispute was resolved by a referendum endorsing Britain leaving the EU.

National leaders had no wish to be held accountable to a popularly elected multi-national parliament. Even though the Treaty of Rome called for the election of a European Parliament, this was not put into effect for two decades. The European Coal and Steel Community had a Common Assembly to represent 'the peoples of Europe'. Representation of electorates was indirect: its seventy-eight members were chosen by members of national parliaments. Since each country's members represented a range of parties, this established an important principle. Instead of MPs sitting in national groups, Assembly members seated themselves with MPs from other countries who shared a similar ideology, whether socialist, Christian or liberal.

When the European Economic Community was created, it had a European Parliamentary Assembly modelled on the ECSC with 142 indirectly elected members. They were first elected by voters to sit in their national parliament, and the national parliament then selected a limited number of its MPs to sit in the European Assembly. In 1962 the institution changed its name to the European Parliament. By 1970 it had some powers over the budget of the European Commission and was campaigning for the direct election of its MPs.

In the absence of a parliament, the ECSC and the European Commission lacked the legitimacy that comes from being accountable to politicians elected by the people they nominally represent. The absence of an elected European Parliament also meant that national citizens did not become engaged with European affairs by political parties campaigning for their votes. When the heads of national governments created the European Council to give themselves more influence over the Commission, they finally gave in to demands from the EP for their members to be directly elected.

A directly elected European Parliament. The direct election of the EP starting in 1979 was intended to strengthen the EU's legitimacy and encourage voters to become more committed to EU institutions and policies. However, the rules for a multi-national election have produced practices significantly different from democratic national elections.

The very unequal population of the EU's member states has undermined the democratic principle of one person, one vote, one value. In 1979 four states had populations of the order of 60 million people, and Spain and the Netherlands were medium-sized, while the population of six states ranged between half a million and 10 million. If members of the European Parliament (MEPs) had been allocated to countries in keeping with the one person, one value principle, then Germany, France, Italy and the UK would each have had about 120 MEPs for every MEP from Luxembourg.

Although each state is required to elect its MEPs by proportional representation, the number of MEPs allocated to each country is by a system of *disproportional* representation (Rose, 2015). The allocation starts by setting the minimum number of MEPs a country can have at six, and placing a ceiling on the maximum number of MEPs; it was eighty-one initially and raised to ninety-six after German re-unification. Electing an MEP in Germany requires up to sixteen times more votes than needed to become an MEP in one of the four countries with six MEPs. Since a big majority of EU member states have a small population, twenty-two states are over-represented in the European Parliament, while the five most populous states are under-represented.

Although direct election has succeeded in giving the European Parliament a claim to legitimacy that it had previously lacked, it has not succeeded in engaging the interest of the peoples of Europe. The turnout of voters is consistently much lower than at national elections. In the 2024 election overall turnout was 51 per cent. It was highest in Belgium, 89 percent, where voting is compulsory, and an important national election is held on the same day as the EP vote. In a majority of countries less than half the electorate voted.

Europeans who vote treat an EP election tend to treat it as a second-order election; they usually vote for the party they support in their national election. Reif and Schmitt (1980) explained this as due to the much greater importance of national issues to voters. Moreover, ballots offer a choice between national parties familiar to voters rather than the unfamiliar names of the multi-national parties in the European Parliament. Populist parties have succeeded in winning more seats in the EP than in their national parliament by campaigning against European integration (Ehin and Talving, 2021). In the last election in which Britons voted, the anti-EU Brexit Party, led by Nigel Farage, returned the most British MEPs.

In order to conduct the affairs of a parliament whose members represent upwards of 150 national parties, MEPs organize into multi-national political groups. Each group must have at least twenty-three members from at least one-quarter of the EU's member states. After the 2024 European Parliament election the largest EP group was the European People's Party, with 188 MEPs, one-quarter of the EP's total membership of 720 MEPs. The Socialist and Democratic Party had 136 MEPs. Populist groups finished third and fourth; Renew, a centrist group, came fifth.

Consulting Europeans within limits. EU treaties make no provision for calling a Europe-wide referendum to seek consent for major decisions. However, each member state can call a referendum on an EU policy and some, such as Ireland, are constitutionally required to hold a referendum on each treaty. Many national governments have asked their citizens to vote in a referendum on joining the EU, and most have given a big endorsement to joining. Norway is exceptional in having its voters twice reject the government's plans to join the EU, and Swiss voters have several times rejected proposals for closer association with the EU (Rose, 2020).

In 2001 the Laeken Declaration of the European Council authorized a Convention to draft a European Constitution intended to make the EU more efficient and bring it closer to its citizens. The great majority of the Convention members were committed to furthering European integration. The text was prepared by a small executive committee chaired by the forceful pro-European former president of France Valéry Giscard d'Estaing (Castiglione et al., 2007). The preamble invoked Thucydides, declaring, 'Power is not in the hands of a minority but of the whole people'. When a small group within the Convention suggested enhancing the Constitution's legitimacy by putting it to a Europe-wide referendum, the Laeken Declaration dismissed the proposal out of hand, declaring, 'European citizens undoubtedly support the EU's broad aims'.

When the draft European Constitution was presented to national governments for approval in 2004, the majority of governments decided to put it to a national referendum for approval. The first two national referendums produced majorities in favour of the Constitution. However, the next two referendums produced the opposite result: in France 55 per cent were against the Constitution, and in the Netherlands 62 per cent. The Constitution failed. The prospect of a national referendum rejecting a treaty has made Europe's governors cautious about a binding popular endorsement to expand their powers.

The EU has sought to show it openness to the views of its citizens by introducing a Citizens' Initiative. However, the rules about the use of the Initiative reflect its resistance to giving citizens a decisive voice, as is the case in many national initiatives. Initiatives can recommend legislation only within the EU's existing powers; they cannot suggest altering its powers. A petition must be signed by 1 million citizens from at least seven EU member states. This favours large multi-national pressure groups that can co-ordinate activities across multiple national boundaries and languages. If a petition is verified as meeting these requirements, it can be presented to a committee of the European Parliament, and the Commission is obligated to provide a reasoned comment. However, the Commission is not obligated to refer the Initiative proposal to Parliament for action nor is Parliament obliged to approve it. The EU receives about ten petitions a year, eight of which are validated and receive replies. The less controversial the subject matter, the more likely it is that a petition will stimulate administrative or legislative action (cf. Longo, 2019).

A directly elected Parliament gives the European Union an essential institution of a democratic state. Yet the European Parliament lacks the full powers of a conventional national parliament. Unique features of the European Union cause a democratic deficit; it cannot hold accountable the European Commission representing twenty-seven national governments for the decisions it makes or frustrates (Rose, 2020: 39). Proposals to increase democratic institutions and procedures, such as directly electing the president of the European Union, are plentiful. However, whatever the effect of institutional reforms, they would not give the EU the security powers of a state.

Foreign affairs without force

Since being founded by treaties creating a Community of six states with limited economic competences, European institutions have greatly expanded their powers. The 1970 Davignon report endorsed federalist aspirations to have the EU speak with one voice on major international issues. The preamble of the 1992 Maastricht Treaty proclaimed 'a new stage in the process of European integration'. To symbolize the change, it adopted a new name for its institutions, the European Union, and all citizens of the EU's member states were automatically given European citizenship. The treaty formally conferred on the EU responsibility for foreign policy and security, a collective good for all twenty-seven member states.

The Maastricht Treaty sought to give the European Union a military capability by calling on member states to make their national armed forces available to the European Union to carry out security measures unanimously approved by the European Council. It declared: 'If a member state is the victim of armed aggression on its territory, the other member states shall have towards it an obligation of aid and assistance by all means in their power.' In recognition of the prior commitment of member states to NATO, Article 42 of the Maastricht Treaty added that this obligation 'shall not prejudice the specific character of the security and defence policy of certain member states'. In the event of an aggression, national governments have the option of calling on the EU for assistance or invoking Article 5 of the NATO Treaty. Doing the latter would not only call other European countries to their aid but also the military force of the United States.

The Treaty of Lisbon in 2007 authorized the post of vice president of the European Commission and High Representative of the Union for Foreign Affairs and Security Policy. The vice president is responsible for the EU's Common Security and Defence Policy (CSDP), which is concerned with border management, terrorism, cyber security and PESCO, the Permanent Structures Cooperation, which includes crisis management missions and civil and military operations. Its website describes the EU as taking a leading role in peace-keeping operations, conflict prevention and the strengthening of global security and peace through diplomatic means. It also co-ordinates an annual review of security and defence policy (www.eeas.europa.eu/eeas/what-we-do-policies-and-actions-0_en).

The Lisbon Treaty created a diplomatic corps, the European External Action Service, to speak on behalf of the EU in more than 100 countries worldwide. Where there is a common EU policy, as in matters related to trade and economic relations, the diplomats can speak with one voice. The EU can and does send Special Representatives to select trouble spots where members tend to have a common interest in maintaining peace, for example, the Balkans and Kosovo, the Sahel region of Africa, and the Caucasus and Central Asia. At any one time it can have up to a dozen missions in the field. It does so as a civilian power rather than as a military power (Keukeleire and Delreux, 2022).

The power of the vice president to act is constrained by the need to have the support of the European Council, whose members are heads of national governments with diverse national foreign policy interests. The formal expansion of EU security powers in treaties does not of itself increase the political commitment of member states to the EU acting collectively. This requires building a super-majority of large and small states to adopt policies within the EU's current powers. To gain additional powers requires unanimous consent to a new treaty by all member states and, in some states a referendum in which a majority of national voters endorse the treaty. If the EU does nothing, it outsources to NATO the making of its security policy.

Where EU interests overlap with those of international organizations, the EU co-operates. While not a member of the World Bank in Washington, the EU shares information about the allocation of their respective funds for projects in developing countries. Countries in the eurozone are also members of the International Monetary Fund (IMF) in Washington. Both organizations monitor economic activities in Europe and can provide financial assistance on strict conditions to a country in financial difficulties. IMF decisions give priority to its international economic role, while the ECB is concerned with maintaining the stability of a European political economy. The EU has enhanced observer status at the United Nations. This gives it the right to participate in its activities but not voting rights in the UN General Assembly or a seat on the Security Council. The one EU member with a permanent seat on the Security Council, France, speaks for the French government not the EU.

The European Union cannot compete with NATO as the major provider of security because it lacks a military force. Hence, more than five-sixths of EU

Table 5.1 Overlapping memberships in EU and NATO

EU and NATO members, 23: Belgium, Bulgaria, Croatia, Czech Republic, Denmark, Estonia, Finland, France, Germany, Greece, Hungary, Italy, Latvia, Lithuania, Luxembourg, Netherlands, Poland, Portugal, Romania, Slovakia, Slovenia, Spain and Sweden.

EU members but not NATO members, 4: Austria, Republic of Cyprus, Ireland and Malta.

NATO members but not EU members, 8: Albania, Canada, Iceland, Montenegro, North Macedonia, Norway, Turkey and the United States.

No membership, 1: Switzerland.

Source: Author.

members rely on NATO for their military security (Table 5.1). In addition, eight countries rely on NATO for their military security while going it alone for their economic security, either in terms of strength like the United States and Norway; economic marginality, Albania; or geography, Canada. Four countries belong to the European Union but have made the political choice to stay out of NATO. Switzerland is uniquely self-reliant for both its economic and military security. European governments not only engage in differentiation in their commitment to EU economic policies but also differentiate functionally between the EU and NATO when seeking security.

Bibliography

Anderson, Christopher J., Blais, André, Bowler, Shaun, Donovan, Todd and Listhaug, Ola, 2005. *Losers' Consent: Elections and Democratic Legitimacy*. Oxford: Oxford University Press.

Artis, Michael J. and Rose, Richard, eds., 2002. 'Currency Choices in an Interdependent World'. *Journal of Public Policy* (special issue), 22, 2, 107–260.

Castiglione, Dario, Schonlau, Justus, Longman, Chris, Lombardo, Emanuela, Borragan, Nieves P.-S. and Aziz, Miriam, 2007. *Constitutional Politics of the European Union*. London: Palgrave Macmillan.

Ehin, Piret and Talving, Liisa, 2021. 'Still Second-Order? European Elections in the Era of Populism, Extremism and Euroscepticism'. *Politics*, 41, 4, 467–85.

Keukeleire, S. and Delreux, T., 2022. *The Foreign Policy of the European Union*. London: Bloomsbury, 3rd edition.

Longo, Erik, 2019. 'The European Citizens' Initiative: Too Much Democracy for EU Polity?'. *German Law Journal*, 20, 2, 181–200.

Reif, Karlheinz and Schmitt, Hermann, 1980. 'Nine Second-Order National Elections: A Conceptual Framework for Analyzing European Election Results'. *European Journal of Political Research*, 8, 1, 3–44.

Rose, Richard, 2015. *Representing Europeans: A Pragmatic Approach*. Oxford: Oxford University Press.

Rose, Richard, 2020. *How Referendums Challenge European Democracy*. London: Palgrave Macmillan.

Thomson, Robert, 2012. *Resolving Controversy in the European Union*. Cambridge: Cambridge University Press.

Wildavsky, Aaron, 1975. 'The Two Presidencies'. In Aaron Wildavsky, ed., *Perspectives on the Presidency*, Boston: Little, Brown, 448–61.

6

The United States pivots to Asia

In the days of sailing ships Europe, especially the British Isles, was the principal source of America's settlers. Initially, immigrants stopped where they landed along the Atlantic coast from New England to South Carolina. That made it easy to maintain trade and personal contacts with Britain and Europe. President Thomas Jefferson's purchase of the Louisiana territory in 1803, an enormous tract of land between the Mississippi River and the Rocky Mountains, stimulated settlers and immigrants to move west. Since the rivers of the Mississippi Valley drained into the Gulf of Mexico, those who went west were moving away from a ready link with Europe.

The Pacific Coast of North America was explored by Spanish fleets based in Mexico and by Russians trading in Alaska. The Texas-Mexican War was followed by Texas and California becoming American states just before gold was discovered in California in 1848. In 1867 the American government purchased Alaska from Russia, and two years later railway tracks linked San Francisco with the American East Coast. The opening of the Panama Canal in 1914 strengthened the ties between the Pacific Coast and East Coast ports. This was followed by the development of interstate highways creating a coast-to-coast link for road transport. In the 1940 census the four most populous American states were still all east of the Mississippi River, with a combined population more than five times that of California.

Along with European countries, the United States established commercial outlets in China in the late nineteenth century; it also sent Christian missionaries into rural China. American ships forcibly opened Japan to trade with the West in 1854. The surprise Japanese air attack on the United States' Pacific fleet at Pearl Harbour brought it into the Second World War in 1941. The United States led the fight against Japan in the Pacific, while European governments surrendered their colonies to Japan. The Second World War was finally concluded after American planes dropped two atomic bombs on Japan in August 1945.

Because it is a world power, the American commitment to European security must be seen in a global context. The next section shows how it first filled a power gap in Asia and now seeks to balance the power of the People's Republic of China (PRC). Throughout the post-war period the percentage of Americans whose families were European immigrants has been contracting and the percentage with roots in Latin America and Asia has been growing. In pursuit of global security, since 1950 the United States has fought five wars in Asia and the Middle East with limited involvement by European states. The cumulative effect of these changes has been described by President Barack Obama, born in Hawaii and a resident of Indonesia in his youth, as a pivot to Asia.

Filling a power vacuum in Asia

Peace creates a power gap. The abrupt end of the Second World War in August 1945 left the United States as the sole power in the Pacific. Japan was defeated and subject to a large American army of occupation. The United States' principal ally, the Republic of China government of Chiang Kai-shek, was losing a civil war with communist forces led by Mao Zedong. European powers with substantial colonies in Asia, such as Britain, France and the Netherlands, were withdrawing from the region, peacefully or after armed conflict with nationalists seeking independence and fighting each other.

The attack on Pearl Harbor showed that the United States could not rely, as it once had, on the Pacific Ocean for military security. The 1947 Japanese Constitution, written under the supervision of American occupation forces, stated in Article 9 that the country renounced the use of force in international relations and would not maintain an army, navy or air force. Unlike Germany, which began re-arming in the 1950s as a NATO member, Japan did not re-arm when new military threats arose three years later in Korea. By 2014, when the Japanese government re-interpreted its constitution as allowing the participation in collective self-defence, it had long been on the sidelines of military security in Asia.

Communist forces won the Chinese civil war in 1949 and established the People's Republic of China (PRC). Chiang Kai-shek's government retreated to the island of Taiwan and maintained that it was still the government of the whole of China. The United States refused to recognize the PRC, albeit five West European countries did so in 1950 and others gradually followed. The change of government in China led to an acrimonious debate in the United States, with Senator Joseph McCarthy leading the charge that the United States had 'lost' China to the Chinese communists. In the 1950s the Soviet Union supplied significant economic assistance to the new Chinese regime. This raised the prospect of the United States, unlike its European partners in NATO, being confronted with communist challenges to its security on two continents.

The United States extended the reach of its security to mainland Asia in 1950 by coming to the military aid of the Republic of Korea when the communist-controlled government of North Korea invaded the south. When American forces pursued North Korean forces close to the Chinese border, the PRC provided military support to North Korea. When the United States engaged in war in Vietnam, it was once again fighting a force supported by the Chinese communist regime. Concurrently, relations between Beijing and Moscow became strained. Mao Zedong's government claimed ideological leadership of global communism, and there were even minor armed conflicts on the Sino-Soviet border.

A new bilateral relationship between the United States and China was created during the presidency of Richard Nixon and Henry Kissinger's time as Nixon's national security adviser. The United States did not veto the PRC taking over the Chinese seat as a permanent member of the UN Security Council, and in 1972 President Nixon made a trip to China to meet Mao. Since then eight American presidents have travelled to China, and Chinese leaders have visited the United States, while relations between Beijing and Washington have oscillated. The constant is that they have been bilateral: European governments have not been involved.

Economic growth fills the power gap. When the Second World War ended, no Asian country was of major importance in the world economy. In 1953 the gross domestic product of China was 2 per cent that of the United States and Japan's was 5 per cent. Even though Japan was much more populous than West

Germany, which had been even more disrupted than Japan by military defeat, the Japanese economy was still only half the size of Germany (Rose, 1991: 245).

Whereas post-war European economies achieved economic growth based on a significant degree of industrialization before the Second World War, Japan and China faced the challenge of creating modern economies from a much lower economic base. Because of the size of their populations – Japan was much larger than any European country and China's population a multiple of the United States – their total GDP was substantial; however, per capita GDP was low by European or American standards. Nonetheless, their large populations meant that economic development could sooner or later make these countries very important in the global economy.

By 1970 Japan had surpassed Germany to become the world's second-largest economy, at almost one-third the size of the United States; by the year 2000 its economy was valued at almost half that of the United States. China, suffering the effects of Mao's Great Leap Forward to a non-market economy, was below Italy in 1970. The decision to become a competitive global economy meant that by 2010 China had become the world's second-largest economy.

Today, the world's ten largest economies are dispersed globally (Figure 6.1). While the American economy still has the world's largest GDP, China and Japan rank second and third in size. Together, China and Japan now have a larger total GDP than the United States. Even though Germany and the UK ranked fourth- and fifth-biggest in 2020, it is only a matter of time before India surpasses them in its national gross domestic product, while remaining far behind in GDP per capita. Collectively, the three Asian countries now have a total GDP half again larger than the European Union.

The impact of China and Japan on the global economy has been due to their reliance on export-led growth. In 1978 Japan ranked third in the global export of goods behind the United States and Germany, while China ranked twenty-first in exports, below eight European countries and five Asian countries (Nicita and Razo, 2021). Chinese trade was radically boosted by President Bill Clinton securing China most-favoured-nation status for trade and admission to the World Trade Organization (WTO). In a March 2000 speech pushing Congress to enact the United States–China Trade Relations Act, Clinton argued that WTO admission would bring big benefits: 'We'll be able to export products without exporting jobs', while China would not be able to exploit valuable American technology. The resulting rise in Chinese living standards

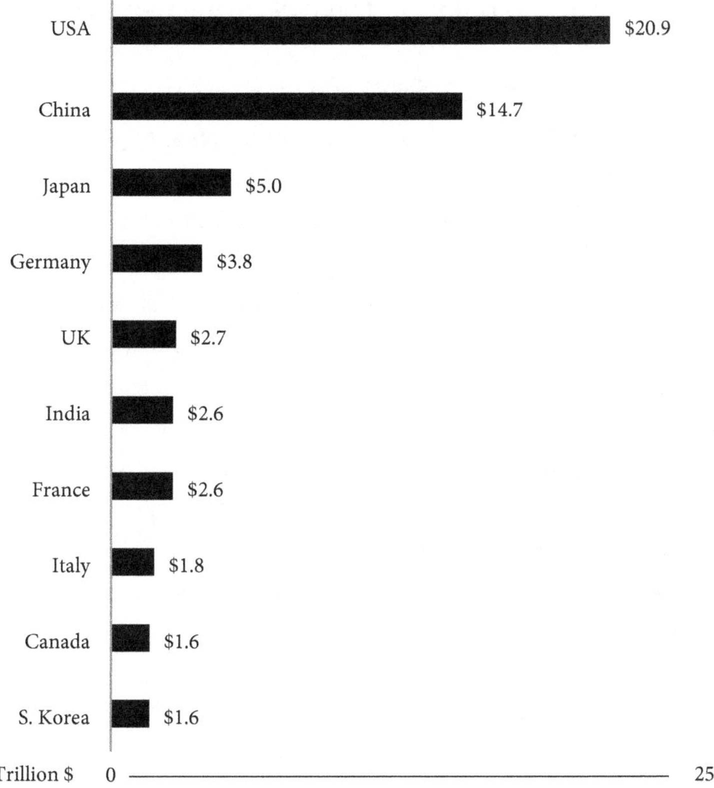

Figure 6.1 World's ten largest economies, 2020

Source: Average nominal value of Gross Domestic Product, 2016-2020. en.wikipedia.org/wiki/List_of_countries_by_largest_historical_GDP.

was expected to promote political liberalization, and 'the more democratic China becomes, the more peaceful it will be in its external behaviour' (quoted in Miller, 2020: 171; cf. Friedberg, 2011).

Optimism about the benefits of trade with China was short-lived; by 2014 the US–China Business Council was citing numerous examples of China not meeting its World Trade Organization obligations. China is now the country that has the biggest surplus of export revenue over imports; in 2020 it stood at more than $400 billion. With total trade in goods with China and ASEAN countries now at $1 trillion, the American economy is truly integrated into Asia. Moreover, an estimated 5 million American jobs have been lost through increased trade with China, and this has had a knock-on effect on American politics.

America's population leaves Europe behind

Immigration in the past. When the first American census was held in 1790, four-fifths of the country's population were immigrants; they themselves or their family had relatively recently come from Europe. In addition one-fifth were Black slaves from Africa. In the century that followed, a combination of European immigration and a high birth rate led to a massive increase in population. The American census just before the First World War recorded the country's population as 88 per cent white, 11 per cent Black, and the remaining 1 per cent as native Americans, Asians or from Latin America.

Tens of millions of European immigrants maintained ties with Europe. In the decade after 1900 more than 7.5 million European immigrants were settled in the United States, principally from the multi-national territories of the Habsburg monarchy, tsarist Russia and Italy. Immigrants from other continents were fewer than one-tenth of the total. Big cities were polylingual as immigrants could use their native language in many contexts, and church membership often reinforced ties with Europe.

Legislation restricting immigration, the Depression and the Second World War reduced the flow of people from Europe to less than one-tenth the previous peak. The passage of time attenuated both family ties with Europe and the number of households where English was not the home language. The decline was hastened by the fact that German and Italian were the languages of enemies of the United States in the Second World War. Turmoil in Europe meant that national boundaries radically changed and distant relatives fell victim to the scourges of war. The continued growth of the United States' population depended primarily on a natural increase among people whose roots were American. The 1950 census reported a population 88 per cent white and 10 per cent Black; the remaining 2 per cent were mostly Hispanic or Asian.

Immigration goes global. Since the Second World War, immigration to the United States has changed in kind. The 1950s was the last decade when the majority of immigrants came from Europe. Since then, the absolute number of immigrants from Europe has declined, and the percentage of European immigrants in the total population has declined even more. The combination of generational turnover and changes in the continents from which immigrants come has eroded American ties with Europe.

In the past half-century more than 41 million immigrants from all over the world have established legal residence in the United States. Almost half the immigrants have come from Spanish-speaking countries in the western hemisphere. Asian countries were the homeland of more than one-third of immigrants, including more than 2.7 million immigrants from China and 2.5 million from the Philippines. Fewer than one-eighth of immigrants have come from Europe (Office of Immigration Statistics, 2021: 8ff.).

In the decade since 2010 a total of 10.6 million immigrants have become legal residents. The largest group, 38 per cent, came from Asian countries. Second in size were immigrants from Latin America, led by 1.5 million from Mexico, followed by El Salvador and Colombia. Europe was the source of only 8 per cent of immigrants (Figure 6.2). The combination of fading family ties with Europe and geographical mobility means that when Californians are asked where they come from, they are more likely to name a Latin American or Asian country than Oklahoma or Illinois.

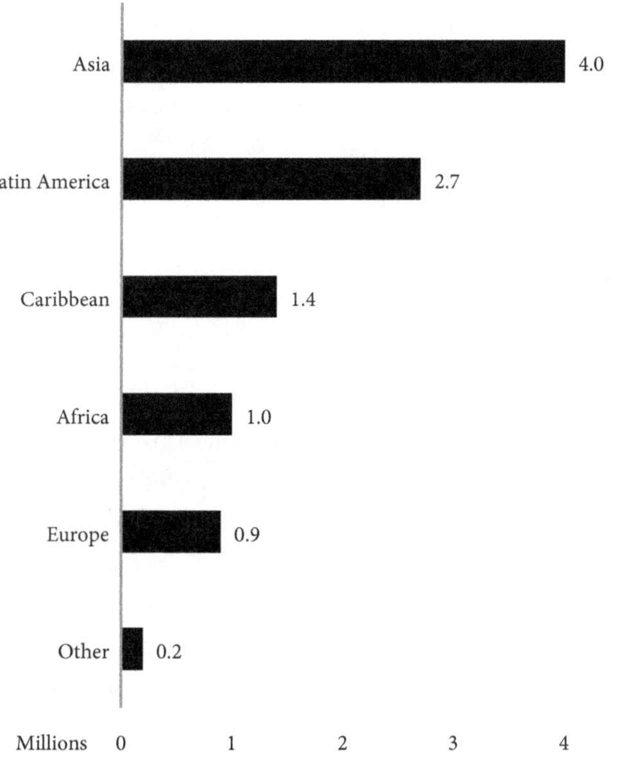

Figure 6.2 Continents of origin of US immigrants, 2010–19

Source: https://en.wikipedia.org/wiki/American_ancestry#.

The US Census no longer collects data about the country of birth of parents, as it did when many respondents were the American-born offspring of immigrant parents. In the 2020 census the only available indicator of European origin is the category of white Americans. Because of the influx of immigrants from other continents, between 1970 and 2020 white Americans fell to 63 per cent of census respondents. Much more relevant politically is the decline in Americans who identify as of European origin. This reflects ethnic intermarriage and the many generations that separate people from their European forebears (Perez and Hirschman, 2009). Unlike immigrants and their offspring, for whom a homeland on another continent is still a lived experience, for Americans of European descent ethnicity is now optional. When the Census Bureau asks people about their ancestry, an increasing proportion of people answer 'American' without any qualification (Prewitt, 2013).

The geographical movement of the American population to the Sunbelt and the West Coast has altered the geography of presidential elections. When Franklin D. Roosevelt ran for re-election in 1940 as Nazi Germany was advancing across Europe, the thirteen East Coast founding states settled from Europe had 187 of the 266 Electoral College votes needed to elect the president. The Sunbelt states of Florida, Texas and Arizona had only thirty-three Electoral College votes, and the three Pacific coast states had thirty-five votes.

Many voters in key states in the 2024 presidential election look to Latin America and Asia rather than Europe. The three Sunbelt states have eighty-one Electoral College votes and the three Pacific Coast states have seventy-four votes. Together these six states have more than half the Electoral College votes needed to win the White House. By contrast, the thirteen states that were European colonies three centuries ago have only two-fifths of the votes needed.

For Europeans the changing composition of the American population means that shared roots and values cannot be relied upon to maintain military security through a North Atlantic alliance. American politicians may exploit their European roots in Ireland or Italy when running for election, but this is irrelevant in the calculations of the president's national security adviser and the Pentagon.

Washington fights wars globally

Since 1945 the United States has not sent troops into action to defend a NATO country. Its policy of deterrence has been effective in maintaining Europe's military security and preventing an armed conflict between two nuclear superpowers. However, as a global power the United States has concurrently had a stake in maintaining security far beyond Europe. It has intervened three times in wars initiated by Asian or Middle Eastern belligerents, and it has initiated two wars in the Near East in efforts to root out perceived threats to American national security.

Five wars from Korea to Iraq. Japan's defeat in the Second World War was accompanied by its loss of Korea, which it had held since 1910. American forces occupied South Korea and Soviet troops occupied North Korea on terms that were initially agreed. However, with the advent of the Cold War, each side backed the division of the Asian peninsula into two states (Cumings, 2005). A government of the Republic of Korea was created in 1948 and a communist regime was created in North Korea. American troops withdrew in 1949.

When communist North Korea unexpectedly invaded the southern half of a divided country in June 1950, the United States had only a few hundred troops in the country. It took the lead in getting the United Nations Security Council to declare the invasion an act of aggression and to authorize member states to provide military assistance to the Republic of Korea. This was possible because North Korea's allies were not present to veto this policy: the Soviet Union was abstaining from participation and the People's Republic of China had not yet been seated. The importance of Korea as a military shield to Japan and the fear that if the invasion was not resisted the PRC would gradually take over the whole of East Asia led President Harry Truman to send American troops to defend the Republic of Korea.

The Korean War quickly became a hot war. While the Soviet Union gave support to North Korea, its troops did not engage with US forces. After American forces under the command of General Douglas MacArthur repulsed North Korean troops from the Republic and pursued them towards its border with China, the PRC reacted by joining forces with North Korea. This resulted in the repulse of American troops back towards the dividing line between North and South Korea, and fighting gradually reached a stalemate. An armistice was signed in July 1953.

The United States committed more than 1,700,000 troops to the Korean War, nine times more than the total committed by twenty-one other countries sending military assistance to the Republic. The UK and Turkey were leaders in sending troops to support the principle of collective security, which was a major justification for the United States sending troops to Europe in the event of Soviet aggression. Limited military preparedness for countering aggression stimulated American policymakers to accelerate building a battle-ready force in the event of Soviet aggression in Europe.

Although European countries had had colonies in Asia for centuries, their capture by the Japanese army in the Second World War and forceful nationalist demands for independence led to their withdrawal from Asia. American interest in Vietnam reflected the view that the global military expansion of communist regimes threatened the national security of the United States. In an April 1954 press conference, President Dwight Eisenhower described a communist takeover of Vietnam as threatening to be the first of a set of dominos that could fall to communism, including the Philippines and Japan, thereby threatening the United States.

President Eisenhower took the first step into embattled Vietnam in 1955, sending American soldiers to train Vietnamese troops. One commitment led to another by four successive presidents. In total the United States sent 3,400,000 troops to Vietnam in an attempt to keep pro-American governments in power In 1973 President Richard Nixon signed a peace treaty with communist forces and American troops abandoned the country.

The United States launched the South-East Asian Treaty Organization (SEATO) in 1954 with the intent of creating an Asian military alliance offering protection against communist China. It brought together Australia, New Zealand, the Philippines, Japan, Thailand, Pakistan, the United Kingdom, France and the United States. SEATO was modelled loosely on NATO, but its members lacked a strong commitment to joint military action. Asian countries tended to give priority to internal insurrections and had no wish to provoke Chinese threats. Australia committed troops to the Vietnam war but neither Britain nor France did. After two decades as a hollow pact, SEATO was disbanded in 1977 (Franklin, 2006).

The Gulf War began in 1990 as a border dispute between a pro-Soviet Iraq government led by Saddam Hussain and Kuwait, an oil-rich country on the Persian Gulf between Iraq and Saudi Arabia. Iraqi military forces overwhelmed Kuwait and occupied the whole of the country, and the United Nations adopted a resolution imposing sanctions on Iraq. European states with interests in the Middle East joined the United States in committing forces; by autumn, 200,000 American troops and 28,000 British and French troops were in the region. As Iraq refused to accept UN conditions to withdraw from Kuwait, the build-up of forces continued until 700,000 American troops were in the Gulf. A military strike followed in February 1991, and within days, Iraqi troops fled Kuwait, with few allied casualties. The United States halted operations rather than invading and overthrowing the Iraqi regime that had started the war.

Al-Qaeda's successful attack on public buildings in New York and Washington on 11 September 2001 created a fresh challenge to national security from a non-state organisation using unconventional force in a *jihad* (violent struggle). As Al-Qaeda operated as a trans-national underground organization, countries that were attacked could not launch a conventional counter-attack. Al-Qaeda did maintain a headquarters in Afghanistan, from which it conducted an ideological campaign against Western states and values. The US Congress passed a resolution authorizing the president to use military force against the organizers of the 9/11 attack, their associates and any source of future attacks. President George Bush declared a War on Terror and issued an ultimatum to the Taliban-controlled Afghan government to surrender the leaders of the Al-Qaeda organization. Bush also invoked Article 5 of the NATO Treaty, which commits all member states to offer assistance to a NATO member attacked on its own soil, as had happened on 9/11.

Since the Afghan state was sheltering a major terrorist organization, the United States launched a military invasion of Afghanistan. The Al-Qaeda leadership found shelter in Pakistan. In keeping with a common interest in being secure against terrorism, more than twenty NATO countries plus dozens of countries scattered across continents formally allied with the United States in the grandiosely named Operation Enduring Freedom coalition. Most provided only logistical support for American planes and ships or sent forces that would not be engaged in military combat in Afghanistan. Britain and France were exceptional in committing troops to action in the field.

The American-led coalition quickly captured the capital, Taliban forces fled to the mountains, and anti-Taliban Afghan groups supported the creation of a new government. The United States made a bilateral agreement with the new Afghan government to keep forces stationed there for use against insurgent groups. On the tenth anniversary of the beginning of the war, 100,000 American troops were in Afghanistan and Osama bin Laden was dead, shot at his hideout in Pakistan by an American special operations team. Twenty years after 9/11, American troops were withdrawn and the Taliban again took control of the Afghan government. Since then, the Taliban regime has tolerated *jihadi* organizations that have engaged in violence in Muslim states but not the United States.

The American invasion of Iraq in 2003 was justified as a pre-emptive strike to prevent the regime from developing nuclear weapons that might in future be a threat to American security. The United States sought and failed to secure United Nations endorsement of its military action in the absence of confirmed evidence of Iraq building nuclear weapons. Doubts about the invasion were widely shared among NATO member states; fewer than half made even a nominal commitment to participate. UK Prime Minister Tony Blair, however, committed 46,000 British troops to fight in Iraq.

The Anglo-American invasion succeeded in toppling Saddam's regime but failed to find convincing evidence that it was developing nuclear weapons. The political vacuum that invasion created did not lead to the creation of a democratic regime, as Washington had hoped. The new regime was caught up in a civil war in which multiple groups competed to claim that they were the rightful state. American forces were involved in counter-insurgency operations until 2011. The 2016 report of the Chilcot Inquiry into the UK's participation in the Iraq war found that the brutal dictatorship of Saddam Hussein had not presented a threat to British security. It thus endorsed the position of France, Germany and other NATO members that did not participate in the war.

National security outlooks diverge. The American pivot to Asia reflects Washington's readiness to see its national security in global terms. Threats are not seen in terms of an invasion from a neighbouring country. The United States has not been invaded by foreign troops since the War of 1812, when British troops captured Washington and burnt the White House. When the Soviet Union showed a readiness to supply Cuba with missiles that could strike the United States, President Kennedy deterred this from happening by warning Nikita Khrushchev that the United States viewed planting Soviet weapons so close to American soil as an act of aggression. The weapons were withdrawn.

Global threats to American security can be constructed in economic terms, such as the role of China in the world economy, or in military terms, as in Russia's armoury of long-range missiles. Within its global security framework, American policymakers see Russia as part of a jigsaw puzzle that includes countries such as China, Iran and Israel, as well as Britain, France and Germany. By contrast, European countries have continued to see their military security as a continental concern. This has resulted in an asymmetry in security perspectives. European countries see NATO as their primary source of military defence, whereas the United States sees Europe as only one among a number of global threats to its security.

Since the Second World War, the United States has had a continuing concern with protecting its national security against a military attack by an Asian power. The North Korean invasion of South Korea in 1950 was resisted on the principle of opposing aggression. The emergence of Japan as a global economy in the 1980s raised concerns about its impact on the American economy. Initially the United States engaged with the People's Republic of China in the mistaken belief that integrating it in the world economy would reduce its interest in military expansion. The United States now seeks to contain trade with China on the grounds that it could put American security at risk. American policy towards Taiwan is a hostage to fortune if China were to try to seize that island.

The United States has long had an interest in the rich oil reserves of the Middle East. Its role as a protector of Israel since that country became independent owes more to American domestic politics than to American national security. Resisting Iraq's invasion of Kuwait reflected a desire both to show that unprovoked aggression does not pay and to protect oil interests in the Persian Gulf. The 9/11 attack on American soil created a threat to American security linked to trans-national Islamist forces, prompting a failed attempt to root out Islamist extremists in Afghanistan. The American invasion of Iraq was motivated by the mistaken belief that Iraq was creating a nuclear threat and the even more mistaken belief that Iraqis would welcome American soldiers as liberators.

Although the UK and France had formerly had global empires and retain an interest in countries on other continents that were once their colonies, they have lacked the military power and the national interest to deter military conflicts involving India and Pakistan or former French colonies in Africa. The United Kingdom has trusted in defending its national security through a special relationship with the United States, sending troops to support American military action from Korea to Iraq. Successive French governments have occasionally supported American military actions when this was deemed in the French interest. However, its unmet ambition has been to achieve Europe's strategic autonomy from the United States. For historic reasons, Germany has not seen military actions outside Europe as threatening its national security. It lost its colonies after being defeated in the First World War and lost its willingness to send troops into action after its military defeat in the Second World War.

Most European governments seek allies because they lack the resources to mount an effective military defence on their own. Since the United States is rich in resources, it is prepared to act alone, but it is also ready to have allies that accept Washington's leadership. For example, the United States often seeks a United Nations resolution condemning aggression because this offers political support. If this is not forthcoming, the United States will still use force and welcome allies in a coalition of the willing. Such support cannot be taken for granted, as shown by European countries abstaining from joining in the Vietnam war. The countries that sent troops to fight alongside the United States in Vietnam were all in the Asia–Pacific region.

European governments are not concerned about the United States pursuing its interests on other continents as long as it protects Europe against aggression. This was achieved during the Cold War by Washington providing military resources to deter the Soviet Union's use of force in Europe. Once the Soviet Union collapsed, European governments were so confident of the continued protection of American forces that they substantially reduced their own commitment of money and materials to collective defence. This practice has now been challenged. The Russian invasion of Ukraine in 2022 has raised the threat of aggression to a level not seen since shortly after the end of the Second World War.

Because the United States is a global power, it is now faced not only with a security threat in Europe but also in Asia from the People's Republic of China. In the 1950s it was able to defend security on two fronts because its resources were far superior. While American resources have not shrunk, the economic and military capacity of China has increased greatly. There is now a political debate in Washington about whether the country should or could simultaneously defend its security in the Pacific as well as Europe. Donald Trump has gone further, questioning whether it is in the American national interest to defend Europe against aggression.

Bibliography

Cumings, Bruce, 2005. *Korea's Place in the Sun: A Modern History*. New York: W. W. Norton.

Franklin, John K., 2006. *The Hollow Pact: Pacific Security and the Southeast Asia Treaty Organization*. Fort Worth: Texas Christian University.

Friedberg, Aaron L., 2011. *A Contest for Supremacy: China, America, and the Struggle for Mastery in Asia*. New York: W. W. Norton.

Miller, Benjamin, 2020. *Grand Strategy from Truman to Trump*. Chicago: University of Chicago Press.

Nicita, Alessandro and Razo, Carlos, 2021. 'China: The Rise of a Trade Titan'. Geneva: UNCTAD, 7 April. https://unctad.org/topic/trade-analysis/development-in-motion.

Office of Immigration Statistics, 2021. *2021 Yearbook of Immigration Statistics*. Washington, DC: Department of Homeland Security.

Perez, Anthony D. and Hirschman, Charles, 2009. 'The Changing Racial and Ethnic Composition of the US Population: Emerging American Identities'. *Population Development Review*, 35, 1, 1–51.

Prewitt, Kenneth, 2013. *What Is 'Your' Race?: The Census and Our Flawed Efforts to Classify Americans*. Princeton: Princeton University Press.

Rose, Richard, 1991. *The Postmodern President*. Chatham, NJ: Chatham House, 2nd edition.

Part Three

Security heats up

7

Vladimir Putin: A Soviet-style European

Russia's relationship with Europe is determined not by geography but by politics; it has been constructed and reconstructed as autocratic rulers have changed. Peter the Great moved the capital of his empire from Moscow, which faced to the Urals and further east, to St Petersburg on the Baltic coast, to gain a window on the West. Vladimir Lenin moved the capital of the Soviet Union back to Moscow to make it more secure from European ideas and armies. Joseph Stalin rejected the Leninist belief that building socialism required revolutions across Europe in favour of a doctrine of socialism in one country.

The Soviet Union, like its tsarist predecessor, had a multi-national population and demanded loyalty from its subjects without reference to their ethnic origins. It claimed to represent a global ideology identified with class not ethnicity. The 1989 census reported that 50.8 per cent of the Soviet population were Russians and the Russian Republic of the USSR was by far the largest republic. Since the break-up of the Soviet Union, people identifying as Russian have constituted four-fifths of the population of the Russian Federation.

Vladimir Putin was born in Leningrad (formerly St Petersburg) a year before the death of Stalin, who left a legacy of a communist party-state that controlled education, the media and travel. It kept European ideas from reaching the residents of the most European of Russian cities (Shlapentokh, 2001). For example, radios produced in Soviet factories were designed so that they could not pick up signals from European broadcasters. The Great Patriotic War, in which Leningrad resisted German forces, was a fact of life in the Putin household. His father walked with a limp from war wounds, his mother nearly died of starvation during the German siege of the city, and his elder sister died of deprivation.

Mikhail Gorbachev's initiatives had the unintended consequence of breaking up the Soviet Union but did not lead the Russian Federation into Europe (see Chapter 4). This meant that Vladimir Putin lost his job as a KGB agent in East Germany but he did not lose his belief in the Soviet Union as the institutional embodiment of the Russian Empire. In a documentary film three months before the invasion of Ukraine Putin declared, 'We turned into a completely different country. And what had been built up over 1,000 years was largely lost, and 25 million Russian people in newly independent countries suddenly found themselves cut off from Russia, a major humanitarian tragedy' (Russian News Agency, 2021).

To describe Vladimir Putin as a nationalist raises the question: What is the nation he identifies with? Putin was born and educated in the Soviet Union, and the KGB in which he served was profoundly dedicated to protecting the Soviet Union against divisive forces of class, ideology and ethnicity. His reading taste when young favoured two German authors, Karl Marx and Friedrich Engels, rather than classic Russians such as Leo Tolstoy and Fyodor Dostoevsky. The *patria* that Putin has in mind when he invokes the Great Patriotic War is the Soviet Union. For Putin, the demise of the Soviet Union was the loss of his homeland.

Europeans and the United States have constructed their view of Russia in very different ways. The French philosopher Jean-Jacques Rousseau asserted that Russians were barbarians who would never be civilized, and Karl Marx, a German, viewed Russia as a barbarous power. The founding Chancellor of the democratic West German state, Konrad Adenauer, shared this view, describing the Soviet Union's control of East Germany as resulting in 'Asia standing on the Elbe' (Neumann, 1999: 82, 99ff.). Left-wing intellectuals in Europe and the United States, dissatisfied with their own political system, served as what Lenin called 'useful idiots'; they endorsed the nominal goals of the Soviet system as leading to a brighter future, and accepted the means employed to transform Russia as necessary to purge its Asiatic legacy. Realists described the Soviet Union as a fourth-world economy with a political system in a class of its own in trying to impose a totalitarian ideal.

An understanding of Vladimir Putin's perception of Europe must start with how his views were initially formed growing up as an ordinary youth in Leningrad when the Soviet Union was not a European country but a one-party state and society. It is followed by an analysis of the security implications of Putin's nationalist outlook, in which the nation was not defined by ethnicity but as the Soviet Union. The concluding section shows how Putin's actions have followed his words, using force to return to Moscow's control territories in Georgia, Crimea and Eastern Ukraine that were formerly part of the Soviet Union.

An ambitious KGB recruit

A normal Soviet boyhood. Vladimir Putin was raised in a Soviet flat in circumstances normal to Russians but not to European visitors to the Hermitage Museum and the Mariinsky ballet. The Putin family had one room in a flat shared with multiple families; it had no hot water, no bathroom and a stinking toilet. It was a house without books or talk of politics. His mother, who had only a few years of schooling, had him baptized without telling his father. Putin enjoyed playing in its stairwell, attacking its many rats with a big stick and learning martial arts to hold his own with bigger boys. His school was a short walk away; he paid little attention to his lessons and was not accepted as a member of the Pioneers, the Communist Party's equivalent of the Boy Scouts. In his self-narrated campaign biography, he describes himself as a youthful hooligan (see Putin, 2000, the primary source for this section).

Reading heroic fiction and watching spy movies changed Putin's life: he developed an ambition to join the KGB, the leading Soviet security agency until the fall of the Soviet Union. At the age of sixteen, Putin went to its local office and said he wanted to join the KGB. He was told that if he really wanted to become a spy he should go to law school and keep his opinions to himself. Putin then applied himself to his studies, choosing to learn German rather than English, and was allowed to join the Pioneers. He was admitted to the University of Leningrad Law School. Soviet law rejected such European legal concepts as the rule of law as simply a tool to protect capitalism. It held that the judiciary should be subordinate to the Communist Party. If an individual expressed disagreement with the current party line, the KGB could arrest the speaker for committing a crime against the state, and indictment was considered prima facie proof of guilt (Pipes, 1993).

Because Leningrad was the Soviet Union's second-largest city and was first in attractions offered to tourists, it received a disproportionate number of European and American visitors. However, its residents knew that being seen talking to Western visitors without official authorization could be considered a crime against the Soviet state. Visitors were therefore shunned, as I know from my own experience in visiting Leningrad in 1976. When I went into a restaurant on my own to order a meal, no waiter would bring me a menu and after an hour I left hungry. When I gave a seminar about that year's American election, the discussant was a Communist Party propagandist who described what I said as false consciousness and told the audience the 'true facts' as laid down by the party.

Putin as a KGB loyalist. The KGB was the heir to traditions dating back to the time of Ivan the Terrible. The primary aim of a predecessor, the *Okhrana*, was to protect the security of the tsar's regime against domestic revolutionary forces. It did this by surveillance, spies and infiltrating disruptive agents into groups challenging the authorities. At one point it even supported Lenin in his fights with moderate revolutionaries. The new Soviet regime's intelligence service, renamed the KGB in 1954, endorsed using aggressive practices, sponsoring *agents provocateurs* and spreading disinformation (Wilson, 2005: 10). Its aim was complementary to that of the Communist Party, which used agitation and propaganda to mobilize support for the regime, while the KGB sought to control individuals who might threaten the stability of the party-state. It also operated outside the Soviet Union to counter opposition in Soviet satellite states and track down dissenters who had fled to the West.

When Putin joined the KGB in 1975 the senior officials who socialized him into the culture and procedures of the institution had been working for the KGB since Stalin's time. His self-description as 'an utterly successful product of Soviet patriotic education' (Putin, 2000: 42) was confirmed when he was assigned to the prestigious counter-intelligence directorate, responsible for controlling signs of dissent from unpatriotic Soviet citizens who questioned whatever was the party line of the moment. In his memoir Putin recounts that as a youthful law graduate he once challenged a plan of action because it was against the law. The veteran KGB officer replied, 'But we have instructions. For us, instructions *are* the main law' (emphasis in the original; 2000: 47).

After further training in foreign intelligence, in 1985 Putin was assigned to collect political intelligence about East German government and Communist

Party officials and their critics. His colleagues were members of the East German state security system. What struck Putin and his wife was how different Dresden was from home: 'We had come from a Russia where there were lines and shortages, and in the GDR there was always plenty of everything. I gained about 25 pounds in weight' (Putin, 2000: 70, 75). I was in Dresden five years before Putin was first there. What struck me was how the rebuilt parts of Dresden were more like a Soviet city than a German city. Visitors were tightly controlled and young people could make a silent protest by listening to Bach organ music in a church on a Saturday night.

In some features the KGB view of Europe was similar to that of the American Central Intelligence Agency. There was an acceptance of the Iron Curtain as a stable division within Europe, one-half protected by the United States and its NATO allies and the other by the Soviet Union and its Warsaw Pact conscripts. Each saw their country as a great power armed with nuclear weapons. For that reason, there was a hot line between the Kremlin and the White House to prevent the launch of nuclear weapons by accident or misunderstanding. Their weapons were for deterrence, not attack. Neither side was prepared to risk starting a Third World War by sending military force to back insurgents within the other's sphere of influence. When Soviet troops were sent to put down the Hungarian uprising against Soviet domination in 1956 and the Czech government's attempt to depart from Soviet guidelines in 1968, the United States did nothing.

The Soviet Union and the United States each viewed the other as a security threat; this helped to maintain the commitment of their allies. Paul-Henri Spaak, one of the founders of the European Union, described Stalin as a progenitor of European institutions, since aggressive Soviet threats provided an incentive to hang together in NATO. Lord Ismay, the first secretary-general of NATO, quipped that its purpose was 'to keep the Americans in Europe, the Russians out, and keep the Germans down' (https://www.nato.int/cps/en/natohq/declassified_137930.htm).

Restructuring Russia's status

A fall in status. The fall of the Soviet Union disrupted Vladimir Putin's KGB career but not his commitment to the ideal of the Soviet Union as a great power. With East Germany no longer part of the Soviet bloc, he returned to a

Leningrad that had lost its name. Since his old law school professor, Anatoly Sobchak, had become mayor of the renamed St Petersburg, Putin got a job promoting foreign investments in the city. Putin's knowledge of German and how to get things done by hook or by crook led to the City Council alleging that he was a go-between in corrupt deals involving tens of millions of dollars (Harding, 2012). When Sobchak was defeated in a bid for re-election, Putin lost his job and moved to Moscow in 1996 in search of a new job. His old connections led President Boris Yeltsin to appoint him head of the Federal Security Bureau (FSB), as the re-organized KGB had become known in the newly established Russian Federation.

The global status of the new Russian state was radically different from that of the country that Putin had served with satisfaction. Instead of being a powerful centralized state in which the leader controlled a command economy and a command polity, it was a weak state. The dissolution of the Soviet Union had reduced its population by upwards of 100 million people, and the introduction of a market economy had created uncertainty among ordinary workers about what their wages would buy in a system in which everything was available at a price.

The disruption of the economy meant that the Yeltsin administration depended on foreign support to manage the transition to a market economy. The American administration of President Bill Clinton offered political and economic support to President Yeltsin on the grounds that Russia was 'too nuclear to fail'. In 1996 Clinton and German Chancellor Helmut Kohl secured Russia's admission to the Strasbourg-based Council of Europe, which promotes democracy, human rights and the rule of law. There was a view that the introduction of democratic institutions would discourage the country from once again becoming a security threat (Mandelbaum, 2016: 52ff.; Herspring and Rutland, 2005). The United States also offered money and technical assistance in the optimistic hope that this would lead to Russia becoming a normal European market economy. However, what is normal in Europe is not *normalno* in Russia.

There was growing Russian disillusion with emulating the United States and West European democracies. A total of 48 per cent of Russians described the break-up of the Soviet Union as one of the most shameful events in the twentieth-century history of Russia. Only 2 per cent considered *perestroika* and the introduction of economic reforms a source of national pride (Levada Center, 2023).

Constitutionally debarred from standing for a third term, President Yeltsin sought to groom a successor who would protect him and his family from the vengeance of a successful opponent pursuing corruption charges. With less than a year left before the 2000 presidential election, Yeltsin appointed Vladimir Putin prime minister in August 1999. This put Putin in line to succeed Yeltsin as president. However, the endorsement was of uncertain value, given that Yeltsin by this time had lost the trust of the Russian public (Rose and Munro, 2002: chapter 4). When Yeltsin resigned as president on the last day of 1999, Putin became acting president. On his first day in office, Putin pardoned Yeltsin and granted him total immunity from prosecution.

Within a month of taking office Putin was confronted with an incursion into the Russian territory of Dagestan by Islamist forces based in Chechnya and bombs exploded in Russian cities killing hundreds of people. An official investigation subsequently declared that the bombs were planted by Chechen terrorists. An unofficial commission, three of whose members were subsequently assassinated, found evidence suggesting that the bombs were likely to have been planted by Russian agents to create a *causus belli* for the Kremlin to attack Chechnya. Putin saw Chechnya as threatening Russia with breaking up like Yugoslavia: 'If it wasn't put down it would mean Russia would cease to exist' (Putin, 2000: 139f.). The Russian government launched an air and ground attack on Chechnya. In the months before the March 2000 presidential election, Putin was leading a military campaign described as protecting Russia against terrorists.

Gaining status and power. When Vladimir Putin won the presidential election in 2000 with 52.8 per cent of the vote against divided opponents, he became the strong head of a weak state. The domestic goal that he repeatedly proclaimed was profoundly ambiguous: to achieve 'the dictatorship of law'. Russia and Putin personally had far more experience of dictatorship than of governing by the rule of law. What the mass of the Russian electorate desired was order, that is, predictability in everyday life. Order is a primary responsibility of the state, whether it is democratically elected or a dictatorship, and the Yeltsin years were seen as a time of disorder. Putin's subsequent success in mobilizing the support of people has owed much to restoring order while allowing Russians more freedom than in Soviet years (Rose and Munro, 2002; Rose, Mishler and Munro, 2011).

In foreign policy Putin's initial goal was to end what he saw as the humiliation of Russia's treatment as a weak state that other countries could ignore; he sought to gain acceptance as a major international power once again (Goldgeier and McFaul, 2003). Gaining respect for the Soviet Union was popular. During the Yeltsin administration more than three-quarters of Russians endorsed the view that Russia should remain a superpower, according to the Levada Center, and 88 per cent endorsed Russia having a superpower status. When NATO began admitting countries that had formerly been part of the Soviet-led military bloc, Putin took no immediate retaliatory action, even though it created a group of NATO members bordering Russia, Belarus and Ukraine (cf. Goldgeier and Shifrinson, 2023). More than that, three new NATO members – Estonia, Latvia and Lithuania – had previously been republics of the Soviet Union.

Where there were common interests, co-operation with the United States was possible. The administration of President George H. W. Bush welcomed order replacing the instability of the Yeltsin period and abandoned the liberal hope of the democratization of Russia in favour of dealing with Putin's government on a realistic basis. Washington shared with Moscow a concern about the emergence of a new superpower, China, with which the Russian Federation shared a Far Eastern border. After his first meeting with Putin, President George H. W. Bush said, 'I looked into that man's eyes and saw that he is direct and trustworthy' (quoted in Mufson, 2015). After the 9/11 terror attack on the United States, the two countries shared a common interest in containing Islamist-inspired terrorists close to Russia's borders and potentially able to recruit supporters among minorities within Russia. The United States and NATO allies muted their criticism about the brutal way in which the Russian military was fighting Chechen separatists.

There were economic incentives for President Putin to seek friendly ties with national governments that were members of both the European Union and NATO. In Putin's first term as president, 40 per cent of Russia's trade was with the EU compared to 5 per cent with the United States. The re-unification of Germany removed Moscow's major bargaining card with Germany. Putin sought to replace dependence on Germany propping up the

Russian economy by making Germany dependent on Russia's rich supply of natural resources.

When Putin became president negotiations had already started with the German Chancellor Gerhard Schröder for a pipeline connecting Russia with Germany. In 2005 an agreement was signed for a 1,200-kilometre Nord Stream 1 pipeline carrying Russian gas across the Baltic Sea to Germany without depending on intermediary countries. Shortly after Schröder left office he took highly paid posts with firms involved in constructing the pipeline, and then with Gazprom, which exported the gas. When the pipeline was opened in a formal ceremony in 2011, German Chancellor Angela Merkel and the Russian president attended. The German government saw increased trade with Russia as boosting European security by giving Russia a stake in the European economy. The Putin administration saw it as a relationship that was not only profitable but also a weapon that could be used to threaten German security.

Regaining Soviet territory

The dissolution of the Soviet Union created fifteen states that were independent with borders recognized in international law. However, the borders were those laid down by the Soviet Union. Notwithstanding the legal independence of these new countries, they remained Soviet territory in Vladimir Putin's mind. Thus, what appeared from a European perspective as the Kremlin's attempts to interfere with independent countries was seen by Putin as maintaining their allegiance to Moscow.

There was a readiness among a number of former Soviet republics to keep up links with Moscow as long as their independence and territorial boundaries were respected. This did not always happen. Putin preferred to have separate bilateral relations with each republic so that he could exploit the advantage of Russia's superior size and its military and economic resources. Where dictators ruled, they were ready to come to terms with Putin as long as he supported their domestic hold on power. This was most notably the case in Belarus. Transnistria, a predominantly Russian-populated part of Moldova, broke away to become an independent state recognized by Moscow but not internationally.

When terrorists attacked the United States in 2001, Vladimir Putin was the first to telephone President George W. Bush and offer support for what he described as an international war on terrorists, with which Russia had long been involved in Chechnya (O'Loughlin et al., 2004). When the United States made use of bases in former Soviet republics in Central Asia to fight Afghanistan, Putin accepted this. The Russian experience with fighting in Afghanistan enabled Putin to see that American engagement there could well prove unsuccessful, thereby discouraging the United States from engaging in further conflicts in the region. This view was reinforced by the unsuccessful American invasion of Iraq.

Occupying Georgia. When the tsarist empire collapsed, Georgia regained its historic independence, but was then annexed as a Soviet republic in 1922. As the Soviet Union was heading towards collapse, the republic of Georgia declared independence in April 1991. In the decade that followed there was political instability, widespread corruption and economic insecurity. There was internal conflict as the regions of Abkhazia and South Ossetia, which bordered Russia, sought to secede and become part of the neighbouring state. Following the Rose Revolution in 2003, a new Georgian government introduced democratic reforms and sought to stabilize its economy. Its foreign policy was strongly pro-Western and its leader, Mikheil Saakashvili, sought Georgian membership in the European Union and NATO (Jones, 2023). In April 2008, President Bush endorsed both Georgia and Ukraine becoming candidates for NATO membership. French and German leaders cautioned that this could provoke Russia.

In summer 2008 fighting broke out between South Ossetian rebels and Georgian forces. When the Georgian army advanced into the region, Russian forces promptly came to the aid of the breakaway group, claiming it was acting to protect Russians wherever they lived. Its troops occupied Georgian cities neighbouring South Ossetia. At the same time, a UN peace-keeping mission in Abkhazia was unable to prevent violence between local and Russian troops leading to Abkhazia declaring independence from the Georgian state. Both of the newly self-proclaimed states are recognized by Russia, on which they are heavily dependent, but not by European states or international law.

The immediate reaction of President Bush and EU leaders was to express concern and call for an end to the conflict. When Russia announced that it had achieved its security objective, French President Nicolas Sarkozy brokered a ceasefire that effectively left Abkhazia and South Ossetia under the control of Moscow. For Vladimir Putin, the military action had done much more than gain the addition of territories with fewer than a million people. It had shown that Russia was no longer subservient to foreign governments in its near abroad and that a divided Georgia was unsuitable to belong to NATO. Since then, internal divisions in Georgian politics have resulted in Saakashvili being ousted and a new party, Georgia Dream, taking office, backed by Georgians who had made fortunes dealing with Russia.

Occupying Crimea. The Crimean peninsula became part of the territory of the Russian tsar in the eighteenth century. After the Soviet Union was founded, it became part of the republic of Russia, even though it was geographically within Ukraine. As such, it provided the major Black Sea base for the Soviet navy. Crimea was administratively transferred to the Ukrainian republic in 1954, but its strategic importance remained unchanged. Following the break-up of the Soviet Union, Crimea became part of the new Ukrainian state. The 1997 friendship treaty between Russia and Ukraine recognized Ukrainian sovereignty over Crimea but also accepted Russia's continued use of its military base. The 2001 census recorded 60 per cent of the Crimean population as Russian, 26 per cent as Ukrainian and 14 per cent as Crimean Tatars, who had settled in the area some eight centuries previously. In 2008 the Ukrainian foreign minister complained that ethnic Russians were being given Russian passports, qualifying them to call on Moscow for military assistance on behalf of citizens living abroad.

In competitive elections in a corrupt political system in which communist practices were sometimes followed, the Crimean region returned a big electoral majority in 2010 for Viktor Yanukovych, who became Ukraine's president and looked to Moscow for support. After the Ukrainian Parliament approved an agreement with the European Union in 2013 that would promote free trade and strengthen the association of Ukraine with the EU, President Yanukovych, acting under pressure from Moscow, refused to give his approval. This led to tens of thousands of protesters camping out in Maidan Square in Kyiv. When security forces sought to disperse demonstrators, violence erupted in major cities with numerous deaths and thousands injured. Yanukovych was forced to resign and fled to Russia.

With the government of Ukraine in turmoil, on 28 February 2014 Russian special forces lacking insignia on their uniforms seized Crimean airports, other strategic locations and the regional parliament of Crimea. It immediately elected a new Crimean first minister who appealed to the Putin government for military protection, which was quickly delivered. The following week a Crimean referendum was called on joining the Russian Federation. When international election monitors sought to enter Crimea to observe the referendum, they were stopped at the border by armed force. The official referendum report said that 95.5 per cent of the ballots endorsed Crimea becoming part of the Russian Federation. Less than a month after the arrival of special forces, Crimea was formally annexed by Russia. The next month armed Russian forces in the Donbas region of eastern Ukraine seized government buildings and proclaimed the independent Donetsk People's Republic and Luhansk People's Republic. A majority of United Nations members voted for a resolution affirming that Crimea was part of Ukraine, eleven voted against, and eighty-two abstained. This was not an obstacle to Moscow making Crimea part of the Russian Federation.

Putin's aggressive measures succeeded in ending the humiliation that he had felt due to the decline in Russia's status without triggering a forceful response by NATO. In asserting Russia's power he had the backing of Russian opinion. In Boris Yeltsin's last year as president 65 per cent of Russians thought that the country was no longer a superpower, more than twice the proportion thinking it still had that status (Figure 7.1). Within eight years Putin's actions had reversed the balance: an absolute majority considered the country to be a superpower. The occupation of Crimea raised the proportion seeing Russia as a superpower to 75 per cent and 45 per cent described regaining Crimea as one of the three achievements in Russian history that gave them most pride.

President Vladimir Putin's view of security is a legacy of the Soviet Union. Putin views Soviet republics that became independent countries as part of Russia's near abroad where it has the right to act to protect itself. When it was occasionally suggested that Ukraine become a NATO member, this idea was dismissed by Washington. After Russian forces occupied two regions of Georgia in 2008, they declared their independence but European countries did not recognize this claim. When Russia seized Crimea, its historic Black Sea naval base, the objections of a corrupt and sometimes pro-Moscow Ukrainian

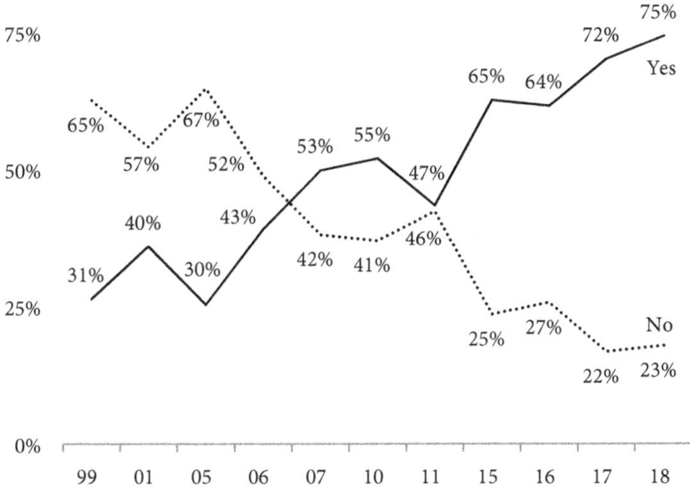

Figure 7.1 Increased pride in Russia as superpower, 1999–2018

Source: Levada Centre surveys. https://www.levada.ru/en/2019/01/25/nationalidentity-and-pride/.

government received little support from Washington. Berlin ignored these military incursions as irrelevant. It described increased economic interdependence as reducing military insecurity, a strategy summed up in the slogan *Wandel durch Handel* (Change through Trade).

Western protests voiced and ignored. The American and European governments did not recognize Crimea's secession from Ukraine. In March 2014 the United States began applying economic sanctions against Russian oil companies, banks and oligarchs whose actions were undermining Ukraine. The sanctions caused a fall in the value of the rouble. However, the measures were well short of the assurances Ukraine felt it had gained in return for surrendering its nuclear weapons to Russia in 1994. A House of Lords Committee noted in 2015 that, as a signer of the 1994 Budapest Memorandum to uphold Ukraine's territorial integrity, 'the British government has not been as active or as visible on this issue as it could have been'. Along with the United States, it sent small groups to train Ukraine's armed forces.

NATO has no commitment to defend Ukrainian territory. The US government reckoned that any move towards offering Ukraine the military protection of NATO would be viewed as a threat to Russia's military security. The policy of President Barack Obama, reacting against unsuccessful American interventions in Afghanistan and Iraq, was to avoid supporting governments that could not defend themselves against their own population. Moreover, the pro-American groups in Ukraine tended to have unrealistic expectations of the support that the United States would offer. Their influence on the Ukrainian government was often countered by the interests of corrupt businesses and politicians profiting from ties with Russia (Goble, 2000).

The European Union dealt with Ukraine as part of its European Neighbourhood Policy but relations were difficult because of divisions within Ukraine between the pro-Russian eastern part and a pro-European western part about giving priority to links with Moscow, where relations were historically strong, or links with Brussels. Bitter fights between leading personalities and parties about who should control Ukraine's government were also an obstacle to co-operation of the sort that had led East European countries to become EU member states.

The ineffectual diplomatic protests that Western powers made encouraged Vladimir Putin to believe that he could continue to use force to reclaim former Soviet territory. Putin directed diplomats to replace conventional discussions about co-operation with an aggressive defence of Russia advancing its territorial interests with force. Russian diplomats learnt that reporting negative international responses to what the Kremlin was doing risked being ignored or treated as incompetent or disloyal. In the words of a BBC commentator (2023), 'Russian diplomacy died under Putin.' What replaced it was reliance on KGB-style means to get what the Kremlin wanted by duplicity, intimidation and force.

Bibliography

BBC, 2023. 'Threats, Insult and Kremlin "Robots"'. https://www.youtube.com/watch?v=v5b24gCarqY. Accessed 3 September 2023.

Goble, Paul A., 2000. 'Establishing Independence in an Interdependent World'. In Sharon Wolchik and Volodymyr Zviglyanich, eds., *Ukraine: The Search for a National Identity*, Lanham, MD: Rowman & Littlefield, 107–20.

Goldgeier, James M. and McFaul, Michael, 2003. *Power and Purpose: US Policy toward Russia after the Cold War*. Washington, DC: Brookings Institution.

Goldgeier, James M. and Shifrinson, Joshua Itzkowitz, eds., 2023. *Evaluating NATO Enlargement from Cold War Victory to the Russia–Ukraine War*. London: Palgrave Macmillan.

Harding, Luke, 2012. 'Marina Salye Obituary, Russian Democrat and Implacable Opponent of Putin'. *The Guardian*, 28 March.

Herspring, Dale R. and Rutland, Peter, 2005. 'Putin and Russia's Foreign Policy'. In Dale Herspring, ed., *Putin's Russia: Past Imperfect, Future Uncertain*, Lanham, MD: Rowman & Littlefield, 2nd edition, 259–92.

Jones, Stephen, 2023. *Georgia: The Conflict with Russia and the Crisis in South Ossetia*. London: House of Commons Library Research Briefing.

Levada Center, 2018. 'National Identity and Pride, 1999–2018'. https://www.levada.ru/en/2019/01/25/national-identity-and-pride/. Accessed 27 December 2023.

Mandelbaum, Michael, 2016. *Mission Failure: America and the World in the Post-Cold War Era*. New York: Oxford University Press.

Mufson, Stephen, 2015. 'Bush Saw Putin's "Soul"'. *Washington Post*, 1 December.

Neumann, Iver B., 1999. *Uses of the Other: 'The East' in European Identity Formation*. Manchester: Manchester University Press.

O'Loughlin, John, et al., 2004. '"A Risky Westward Turn": Putin's 9–11 Script and Ordinary Russians'. *Europe–Asia Studies*, 56, 1, 3–34.

Pipes, Richard, 1993. *Russia under the Bolshevik Regime*. New York: Knopf.

Putin, Vladimir, 2000. *First Person: An Astonishingly Frank Self-Portrait*. New York: Public Affairs Press.

Rose, Richard and Munro, Neil, 2002. *Elections without Order: Russia's Challenge to Vladimir Putin*. Cambridge: Cambridge University Press.

Rose, Richard, Mishler, William and Munro, Neil, 2011. *Popular Support for an Undemocratic Regime: The Changing Views of Russians*. Cambridge: Cambridge University Press.

Russian News Agency, 2021. 'Putin Calls Dissolution of USSR Tragedy and "Collapse of Historical Russia"'. https://tass.com/politics/1374355. Accessed 30 September 2023.

Shlapentokh, Vladimir, 2001. *A Normal Totalitarian Society: How the Soviet Union Functioned and How It Collapsed*. Armonk, NY: M. E. Sharpe.

Wilson, Andrew, 2005. *Virtual Politics: Faking Democracy in the Post-Soviet World*. New Haven: Yale University Press.

8

Ukraine: A proxy war for Europe

The Cold War was a period of cold peace. It was peaceful inasmuch as there was no military combat between NATO and Soviet-led forces. When Soviet troops went into action, they did so to suppress their nominal allies in Warsaw Pact countries. The peace was stable because there was a mutual understanding in Moscow and Washington that, if either side sent troops across the Iron Curtain, this could start the Third World War. The Cold War ended with the collapse of the Soviet Union. The resulting instability was a time of hope. Even if this was not the end of history, European governments tended to see it as the end of the threat of another world war in Europe.

The Russian invasion of Ukraine in February 2022 destroyed the hope that Europe was free from the curse of war. The hundreds of thousands killed and wounded in the battlefields and cities of Ukraine are witness to that. This chapter is being written during the third year of the war and the outcome is uncertain. In a sense, Vladimir Putin has already lost his war aim: the quick integration of Ukraine into the Russian state with a minimum of conflict. Instead, he has united often divided Ukrainians to fight to defend their country from Russian invaders.

The invasion has produced an unprecedented response: the United States and European states have treated Russian aggression as a proxy war against themselves. While Ukraine is not a member of NATO, four countries have land borders with Ukraine and five more have borders with the Russian Federation. For the European Union, Ukraine is no longer a state kept at arm's length in the near abroad (cf. Christiansen et al., 2000). It is fighting a war for the defence of the EU's member states against attacks from Russia. The US and national governments of Europe have sent tens of billions in military supplies and financial assistance to augment the manpower that Ukraine is mobilizing to defend its territory. Combat troops have not been sent. This restraint reflects a desire to avoid full-scale conflict between two nuclear-armed powers, Russia and the United States.

The return of war to Europe has shown that the European Union's increased influence on the continent's economic security cannot compensate for the lack of an armed EU force. Ukraine must rely on national governments, led by the United States, for the military hardware it needs. The European Union has used its institutional resources to co-ordinate the response of national governments to Ukraine's request for aid. The Russian weaponization of its energy exports to Europe has been met by placing sanctions on the rouble and on Russian oligarchs who have made fortunes supporting Putin.

While countries across Europe and the North Atlantic have seen the threat to their security rise, their national resources for defence differ substantially – so does their political will. National governments have a trio of political choices. They can deal with threats on their own, they can co-ordinate actions through the European Union, or they can look to the United States as the hegemonic leader of NATO. Since the Russian invasion of Ukraine, some European governments have done all three.

The invasion has established a new Iron Curtain running from the Black Sea to the Baltic. The next section describes how Ukraine has long been fought over as a borderland between Russia and Europe. Vladimir Putin's special military operation to make Ukraine once again subject to Moscow is then examined. Putin miscalculated: he united a much divided Ukraine into opposition to Russian invaders. The invasion has also brought Ukraine much closer to Washington. It has reminded American leaders that as a global power the United States has a stake in European as well as Pacific security. The EU and national governments in Europe, which had previously treated Ukraine as a part of its near abroad, are now offering it support in a proxy war in defence of Europe.

Ukraine: A land trampled on by many feet

The term 'Ukraine' is derived from an old Slavic word meaning borderland. In the course of millennia it has been a home to diverse peoples: from the east Mongols, from the north Lithuanians, from the west Poles and from the south peoples of the Ottoman Empire. Slavs began to settle there in the first millennium, and by the ninth century Kievan Rus was a major empire covering much of present-day Ukraine, Belarus and western Russia. This empire fragmented under weak rulers and was finally destroyed by Mongol invaders in the thirteenth century. For the next six centuries, authority was exercised over parts of the land by a number of rulers, including the Polish-Lithuanian Commonwealth, the Ottoman Empire, the Cossack Hetmanate, the Kingdom of Galicia, the Habsburg Empire and tsarist Russia.

When the tsarist empire collapsed in 1917 a Ukrainian People's Republic was proclaimed by Ukrainian nationalists but failed to survive the civil war between Bolsheviks and their opponents. The outcome was the creation of the Ukrainian Soviet Socialist Republic within the nominally federalist Soviet Union. This resulted in Ukraine having a large number of devolved administrative institutions that were politically integrated with Moscow under the direction of the Communist Party of the Soviet Union. Although it was not an independent state, the Ukrainian republic became a founder member of the United Nations as part of a successful Stalinist move to magnify Moscow's voice in the UN General Assembly. Stalin cited the British Empire as an example of a country having multiple UN members. Ukraine became an independent state only after its communist leaders collaborated with Boris Yeltsin in breaking up the Soviet Union in 1991 to their own advantage.

Whatever its sovereignty or lack of sovereignty, Ukraine has never been a nation state. The authority of its rulers was not based on ethnic identity but on power. The fact that it had a Slavic population did not make it Russian, since many populations between Kyiv and Prussia are Slavic. Shifting borders meant that the ethnic mix of the population has varied over time and remains mixed today.

Soviet experience in a bloodland. The Soviet Union stressed a socialist rather than a national identity. Yet its founders did not conflate Soviet and Russian identities. In recognition of the fact that it took time to develop a common identity among an ethnically heterogeneous population, the state collected data on the nationality of its subjects. In the first all-Union census of 1927, Russians were only 52 per cent of the Soviet Union's population. Ethnic Ukrainians came second with 21 per cent of the Soviet population, millions of whom lived in other republics than Ukraine. In a complementary fashion, residents of Ukraine included millions of Jews and Russians.

Ukraine was the major bloodland in Europe between 1931 and 1945, that is, a land where millions of people were killed for political reasons (Snyder, 2010). The killings started with the *Holodomor* (Ukrainian for death by hunger). Hunger was not due to crop failures but to a policy initiated by Joseph Stalin with the double purpose of collectivizing Ukraine's rich agricultural land and dispossessing kulaks, the class enemy who owned the land. An estimated 3 to 4 million people, more than one-tenth of the Ukrainian population, starved to death. Because the famine was a consequence of the policy of the Soviet state, Ukrainians consider it an act of genocide.

The 1939 Nazi-Soviet pact led to the dismemberment of Poland, and territory with a predominantly Ukrainian population was added to the Ukrainian Republic. When the pact broke down and Hitler's troops invaded Ukraine in 1941, many villages welcomed German troops as liberators from Soviet oppression. On the principle that my enemy's enemy is my friend, some nationalists allied with Germany in hopes of gaining an independent Ukrainian state. German forces recruited nationalists to assist in killing Soviet troops loyal to Moscow, Ukraine's Jewish population and Poles (see e.g. Steinhart, 2015). German suppression of the population resulted in the majority of its people fighting on the Soviet side. Approximately one-fifth of what was then the population of Ukraine is estimated to have been killed. The massive displacement of Poles and the extermination of Jews reduced the republic's ethnic diversity but did not end it.

As the second most populous Soviet republic with natural resources and a high level of human capital, Ukraine and Ukrainians became increasingly integrated in the Soviet system politically and economically. Ukraine's large and rich farmland made it a major source of foodstuffs for the Soviet market. It was a major location for nuclear weapons and its nuclear power plant at Chernobyl was the site of the world's worst nuclear disaster in 1986. An estimated 8 million people who identified as Ukrainians resided in Moscow and other parts of Russia. Before becoming Soviet leader, Nikita Khrushchev had been a commissar in Ukraine promoting a policy of integration through Russification. Leonid Brezhnev, a successor as Soviet leader, was a native of Ukraine and favoured integration too. The use of Russian in official documents, in the media and as a *lingua franca* throughout the Soviet Union encouraged bilingualism among people speaking Ukrainian as their native language.

An independent Ukraine. Ukraine became an independent state for the first time only after Communist leaders collaborated in breaking up the Soviet Union in 1991 and seizing power and property for themselves (cf. Szporluk, 2000). Independence was endorsed by 92 per cent of voters in a December 1991 referendum in Ukraine, and there were majorities in favour of independence in regions with a predominantly Russian ethnic population such as Crimea. The change in political institutions did not make Ukraine a nation state. The final Soviet census identified Ukraine's ethnic population as 73 per cent Ukrainian, 22 per cent Russian, and 5 per cent other. The number of people reported as Russian in the census has since declined as some emigrated and others switched to identifying themselves as Ukrainian (Stebelsky, 2009).

Sovereignty gave the new government in Kyiv the opportunity to open direct communication with national governments in Europe as well as with the European Union and the United States. However, it did not sever the many ties, economic, social and political, that Ukraine had with the newly independent Russian Federation.

Competitive elections have been held regularly since independence, and control of government has changed hands between rival candidates; these are two important criteria of a democratic polity. However, international election observers have repeatedly noted irregularities in the electoral process. Freedom House has characterized Ukraine as a partly free democracy, with widespread corruption, attacks on the media including the assassination of a leading anti-corruption journalist, and inadequate policing.

Changes in control of government have been caused by street protests as well as elections. The victory of the government-sponsored candidate Viktor Yanukovych in November 2004 led to massive street protests, and the Ukrainian Supreme Court annulled the result. In a re-run election held under careful monitoring, the winner was the opposition candidate, Viktor Yushchenko, who had been subject to poisoning during his campaign. However, Yushchenko's administration became mired in corruption and infighting, and he came fifth in his bid for re-election. When the winner, Yanukovych, subsequently refused to sign a EU free-trade agreement approved by the Ukrainian Parliament but opposed by the Kremlin, protests again erupted in 2013, forcing Yanukovych to resign. The ex-president now lives in Moscow. His successor, Petro Poroshenko, was a staunch Ukrainian nationalist with pro-Europe rather than pro-Moscow views. He was also a billionaire oligarch, who presided over a government that failed to prevent the breakaway of pro-Russian regions in eastern Ukraine. In 2019 a television comedian with no previous political experience, Volodymyr Zelensky, won 73 per cent of the vote running on an anti-corruption platform (Shuster, 2024).

In common with other successor states of the Soviet Union, the government of Ukraine has been plagued by corruption; changes in control of the presidency have done little to alter this. On the Corruption Perceptions Index of Transparency International (www.transparency.org), it has consistently been in the more corrupt half of the world's nations. In 2021, two years after Volodymyr Zelensky became president on a platform of cleaning up government, Ukraine ranked 136th among 180 countries, three Index points below Russia. The war has prompted a government drive against corruption affecting its fighting capacity. In the 2023 corruption Index, Ukraine ranked ten points above Russia and 104th worldwide, tied with Serbia and Algeria.

Putin miscalculates

In July 2021, Vladimir Putin signalled his aggressive intent in the article titled 'On the Historical Unity of Russians and Ukrainians'. He stated that Russians and Ukrainians are 'one people' and that Ukraine 'never had a tradition of genuine statehood' (cf. Snyder, 2010). Putin demanded that NATO sign a treaty that would forbid Ukraine or any former Soviet state from joining NATO and end all NATO activity in Eastern Europe. Putin threatened an unspecified military response if NATO maintained what he characterized as its aggressive line.

European leaders were divided about how to deal with evidence that Vladimir Putin was preparing to invade Ukraine. President Emmanuel Macron of France flew to Moscow to entreat President Putin to halt military threats against Ukraine. German Chancellor Olaf Scholz engaged in talks with the Kremlin and warned Putin that sanctions would be imposed should Russia invade Ukraine. Scholz also suggested to Ukrainian President Volodymyr Zelensky that he could avoid Russian belligerence by declaring neutrality and renouncing aspirations to join NATO. Zelensky refused because he did not think Putin could be trusted to respect a country's neutrality.

The view from the Potomac was more accurate. In early December 2021 the Central Intelligence Agency released satellite photos of tens of thousands of Russian forces massing on the Ukraine border and forecast that up to 175,000 Russian troops would be prepared to invade Ukraine in the New Year. In the following month President Joseph Biden cautioned Putin that it would support Ukraine if it were invaded. British Prime Minister Boris Johnson declared that a Russian invasion of Ukraine would be a 'painful, violent and bloody disaster'. In the light of what NATO had not done when Russia invaded Georgia and seized Crimea, Putin took no heed of these warnings.

Putin believed that the majority of Ukrainians would welcome integration into his Moscow-led government. There were common Slavic ties, Russian had been the official language of Ukraine until after the dissolution of the Soviet Union, and one-quarter of the population did not identify themselves as Ukrainians. Their economies were significantly linked, and Russia was Ukraine's principal source of energy. After adjusting for purchasing power parity, the Russian economy was up to eight times larger than Ukraine's, and GDP per capita was more than double that of Ukraine. Ukrainian politicians were divided on multiple grounds, including their attitudes towards Russia and towards association with Europe. Unlike Russia, the government was also weak: it had been overthrown by protests in 2014, and Volodymyr Zelensky had won election as an anti-establishment outsider campaigning against the failure of governors of all parties.

No quick victory. When President Putin launched an invasion of Ukraine, the aim was to win a quick victory by landing Russian paratroopers at an airport in a Kyiv suburb and then seizing the national capital, thereby decapitating the Ukrainian government. Putin used KGB language to describe the invasion as intended to demilitarize and de-Nazify the government of a state that he thought had no right to exist (Shevtsova, 2020). Putin appeared to believe that once Kyiv was seized, pro-Moscow politicians and oligarchs would be ready to participate in a new government and that a decapitated Ukraine leadership would be unable to resist (Pukhov, 2024). Forewarned by the American CIA of the Russian airport attack, Ukraine's military engaged Russian paratroopers there, rendering it useless as a base for Russia seizing the capital.

The Kremlin's previous experience of regaining territories did not prepare Putin for what his actions triggered. The failed capture of Kyiv left the government in the hands of Ukrainians and produced an unexpected political unity among previously divided Ukrainian politicians and people. Ukraine successfully mobilized a force of upwards of half a million and placed a ban on all men under the age of fifty leaving the country so that they could contribute to an all-out war effort. Ukrainian forces have demonstrated that when given Western arms they are fully capable of preventing the advance of Russian troops as the Kremlin had planned. Moreover, European governments and the United States have provided arms and money to support Ukraine's resistance.

While Ukrainian resistance stopped Russian forces from winning a quick victory in the first year of the war, Russian troops have succeeded in the second year of the war in defending territory they have seized from Ukraine. The Russian army is a large but motley collection of career soldiers, privately recruited and financed forces, and convicts offered a chance to gain a pardon for their crimes if they fight in Ukraine. By the third year of the war it enjoys the advantage of having more soldiers and more firepower than Ukraine.

Putin has used state-controlled media and KGB tactics to give ordinary Russians a very one-sided view of the war. The war has been dressed up as a patriotic fight to protect Russia against its chief enemies, the United States and NATO. The 350,000 deaths and injuries suffered by Russian troops have not led to massive protests. Russian public opinion surveys consistently show support for the war. The independent Levada Center (2024) found that 78 per cent of Russians supported the country's military action in Ukraine and 77 per cent thought that Russia would win. When asked whether they favoured continuing the war or starting peace talks, 40 per cent favoured continuing military action against 52 per cent favouring negotiations to end the war, which most assumed would allow Russia to keep control of the Crimea and eastern Ukrainian territories it had annexed. Few Russians endorsed ending the war if it meant giving territory back to Ukraine.

Western allies have sought to impose economic and diplomatic costs on Russia in an attempt to reduce elite and popular support for its continuing military action in Ukraine. In total, Russia is currently the object of more sanctions than any other country in the global economy (Mills, 2024).

The impact of Western economic sanctions has been to turn Russian trade to China, India and Middle Eastern countries not committed to EU and American sanctions. The boost that the war gave to oil and gas prices has increased Russia's revenue from exporting energy. Payments to banks not subject to sanctions can be used to import war materials produced by non-Western countries and from countries that have bought sanctioned war materials to resell them to Russia. The heavy demand for war materials has boosted production in what had been a lagging sector of Russia's economy (eu-solidarity-ukraine.ec.europa.eu/eu-sanctions-against-russia-following-invasion-ukraine_en). Moreover, Russia's dictatorship can allocate resources to produce military equipment without the delays that occur in the 27 EU member states or in Washington.

The failure to achieve a quick Russian victory in Ukraine has not led President Putin to reduce his war aims. In his December 2023 state-of-the-union phone in, Putin told questioners that Ukraine was inherently weak and could only resist Russia with the help of Western countries, whose support would run out sooner or later. He stated that Russia's goals remained the same: demilitarization (that is, Ukrainian disarmament and rejection of engagement with NATO) and de-Nazification (installation of a Ukraine government that looks to Moscow rather than Brussels or Washington). Putin also claimed additional territory currently part of Ukraine such as Odesa. He summarized his revised war aim: 'There will be peace when we achieve our goals.'

The prospect of a prolonged war has frustrated Ukraine's allies in Europe and Washington, creating signs of fatigue in maintaining aid for as long as it takes Ukraine to regain territory now in Russian hands. The Kremlin is looking for such fatigue to reduce the support Ukraine is now receiving from Western allies and hoping the 2024 American presidential election will produce a shift in American foreign policy leaving Russia pre-eminent in Ukraine.

Kyiv has two war aims. Firstly, it wants to defend the territory it now holds against further Russian aggression. Secondly, it wants to regain by force territories in eastern Ukraine and Crimea that Russia now holds. The political pre-condition for achieving both aims is that the United States and European allies continue to provide the military equipment and money needed to achieve these goals.

Washington defends Ukraine up to a point

Until Ukraine became an independent state it was only of interest in Washington as a region of the Soviet Union. Among Ukrainian immigrants to the United States, many were Jews who had fled from pogroms there and had no love for that land. Following the break-up of the Soviet Union, Washington's immediate objective was to prevent the proliferation of nuclear weapons, a goal shared by Moscow. In Soviet times the third-largest stock of nuclear weapons in the world was in Ukraine. Pressure was put on the new Ukrainian government to hand over its nuclear weapons to the Yeltsin government in Moscow. The 1994 Budapest Memorandum gave Russia the nuclear weapons of Ukraine in exchange for a Russian pledge that its territorial integrity would be respected. The pledge proved to be worthless.

Ukraine becomes a test of deterrence. Both the United States and Ukraine have vacillated about NATO membership (NATO, 2024). When the Ukrainian government applied to join NATO in 2008, this was initially endorsed in principle by President George W. Bush, but it so divided the Ukrainian Parliament that its meetings were suspended for more than six weeks. It also divided NATO members, whose unanimous approval is required to accept a new member. Following the Russian invasion of Georgia, US policy shifted away from a commitment to send American troops to Ukraine in the event of a Russian invasion. Following the victory of a pro-Russian candidate in the 2010 Ukrainian presidential election, the new government adopted a policy of being a non-aligned country.

The Russian seizure of Crimea led President Poroshenko to revive a request to join NATO, which the Ukrainian parliament endorsed by a vote of 303 to 8. This was followed by Ukraine receiving $3.4 billion of military equipment and training from the United States and formal recognition by NATO that Ukraine was aspiring to become a member state (Bureau of Political-Military Affairs, 2023). After Volodymyr Zelensky became president, the government increased efforts to be accepted into NATO, and opinion polls indicated that three-fifths of Ukrainians favoured joining NATO (Sasse, 2023: 34). In response to the Kremlin's disapproval of its membership, the secretary-general of NATO has stated, 'Russia has no say in whether Ukraine should be a member of the Alliance.'

The full-scale Russian invasion of Ukraine is critically testing what happens if deterrence fails and war breaks out. Even though Ukraine is not a NATO member, there is widespread recognition that if Russia were successful in Ukraine this would encourage it to attack a NATO member state. This fear is especially strong in the Baltic states bordering Russia. In December 2023 NATO launched Operation Steadfast Defender, its largest military preparedness action since the end of the Cold War. It involved more than 90,000 troops with supporting aircraft, armoured vehicles and ships in a full-scale test of NATO's capacity to mobilize forces scattered across Europe to stall a Russian invasion of a Baltic state.

The Russian attack has given fresh impetus to Ukraine's desire to join NATO. The 2023 NATO summit in Vilnius endorsed Ukraine's future membership on condition that Ukraine continued to reform its democratic and security institutions and made its military capable of acting as part of a multi-national NATO force. It would then extend an invitation to Ukraine to join the alliance 'when allies agree and conditions are met'. The communique's language calls attention to the problematic nature of allied agreement as well as to Ukraine's problematic capacity to reform its institutions.

Ukraine caught in the crossfire of American politics. Since President Harry Truman established the principle in 1947 that the military security of the United States depended on what happened on other continents, American politicians have treated its national interest and European security as two sides of the same coin. Nonetheless, because the White House sees Europe within a global context, Ukraine must today compete for the attention of American policymakers in a multi-polar world in which strategic security threats are also perceived from China and Iran.

The White House lacks the political bandwidth to give priority to security threats worldwide. In spring, 2024 the president and his leading national security officials were simultaneously facing demands for their attention not only from Ukraine but also from the Israel-Palestine conflict, Iran-assisted terrorist attacks on Red Sea shipping, and tensions between China and Taiwan. Three-quarters of Americans polled think all these conflicts are important to America's national interests (Pew, 2024). However, the decision by President Donald Trump to reduce the country's military capacity from that required to fight two wars simultaneously to a single war makes American commitment to the defence of Europe problematic if military challenges occur on two continents simultaneously (Boyes, 2024).

The Biden administration has been forthcoming in supporting Ukraine. As of January 2024 the government has committed the equivalent of $67 billion in military, financial and humanitarian aid to support Ukraine's war effort (IfW, 2024). Of this total, three-fifths pays for military supplies such as tanks and rocket shells. Global shortages of supplies, especially ammunition that is rapidly consumed, have meant that delivery of weapons is lagging behind their formal commitment in an Act of Congress. Moreover, action by Congress lags behind White House promises of aid.

As the war has continued, US public opinion about helping Ukraine has wavered. Weeks after the war started, the Pew Center found that 74 per cent of Americans were positive about giving arms and economic assistance to Ukraine's war effort. By December 2023, the proportion endorsing the amount of aid being sent Ukraine had fallen to little more than three-fifths of respondents (Whiteley, 2024). As for the future, 57 per cent of Americans have favoured sending arms to Ukraine until it reclaims all the territory that Russia has captured. However, 39 per cent have endorsed the alternative: 'The United States should encourage Ukraine to negotiate with Russia to end the conflict, even if it means allowing Russia to keep territory it has captured in Ukraine' (Smeltz and El Baz, 2023).

Division between the White House and a Congress controlled by opposing parties threatens aid to Ukraine. The tens of billions of dollars that President Joseph Biden has sent Ukraine required approval by a majority vote of both the House and the Senate. When Russia invaded Ukraine the Democratic Party had a majority in the House, but since January 2023 the Republican Party has had a majority there. House Republicans see support for Ukraine as competing for money with other policies more popular with their voters and use Biden's requests for aiding Ukraine as a bargaining card. Thus, a $61 billion aid bill for Ukraine was held up for four months at the beginning of 2024 while the Republican Speaker of the House sought to appease diehard party opponents of any further aid to Ukraine. The speaker only put an aid bill to the vote after intelligence briefing that withholding aid could lead to a Russia victory for which he would be blamed. The bill passed with Democrats giving almost unanimous support and Republicans almost evenly divided.

In a joint press conference with President Zelensky in December 2023, Biden scaled down his original pledge of supporting Ukraine 'as long as it takes' to supporting Ukraine 'as long as we can'. While the outcome of the 2024 American presidential election does not depend on the candidates' policies towards Ukraine, it has consequences for aid to Ukraine given the partisan division about American aid. Whereas 62 per cent of Democrats think the United States should continue assisting Ukraine even at some cost to the United States, 66 per cent of Republicans think it should urge Ukraine to seek peace even at some cost to Ukraine (Smeltz and El Baz, 2023). Moreover, whoever is president, White House attention is likely to continue shifting away from Europe and towards China's challenge to America's global power.

European governments do as they do

The European Union describes the goal of its policy as strategic autonomy, that is, giving member states the capacity to act collectively to defend themselves without depending on non-member states, a barely coded reference to avoiding dependence on the United States (Gstöl and Schunz, 2022). This reflects a long-standing French government ambition to lead a European security force independent of Washington. This has been furthered by the concern about Washington's commitment to Europe since Donald Trump entered the White House. In 2017 German Chancellor Angela Merkel said after meeting President Trump, 'We Europeans must now take our fate into our own hands. We have to know that we must fight for our future on our own' (Kaufmann, 2023). However, bold actions have yet to follow these bold words.

The European Union brings defence ministers of member states together to take small steps to reduce the fragmentation of national defence efforts by sharing information and adopting joint projects. A European Defence Agency was established in 2004 to promote co-operation between ministries of defence in developing and purchasing equipment for their national armed forces in a single European market. In 2016 the EU created a small European Defence Fund to make military equipment of different countries operate to common standards so that it could be shared in field operations. In 2017 it adopted a policy for Permanent Structured Co-operation (PESCO) in fields such as cyber security.

The European Union sidelined. The EU's High Representative for Foreign Affairs and Security Policy has concentrated on foreign affairs. Words are the chief resource for foreign affairs diplomacy. For example, they can be used to call for the peaceful settlement of a civil war in Africa. They need not specify what EU actions, if any, will follow. The Ukraine war has been a shock to Europe's governors: it has made deterring military aggression a high priority. This requires armed forces controlled by EU member states. In the absence of an EU military force, Brussels has been sidelined. Major decisions about European defence are made in Washington, Kyiv and Moscow. When describing European policy towards Ukraine, EU officials distinguish two types of actions. The Vice President for Security Affairs can make verbal condemnation of Russian behaviour. Actions that move money and war materials to Ukraine are the responsibility of national governments. Major decisions about European security are made in Washington, Kyiv and Moscow not Brussels.

Immediately after the Russian invasion of Ukraine, the EU adopted a Strategic Compass policy to strengthen its security and defence by 2030. The Compass uses diplomatic resources to analyse security threats and advises on European factories being unable to meet the increased demand for military equipment and munitions. In addition, it has authorized the creation of an EU Rapid Deployment Capacity Force of up to 5,000 troops to act in a crisis situation.

The EU has provided financial assistance to Ukraine within the substantial constraints of a total budget limited to about 1 per cent of the collective GDP of member states. Because it is a seven-year budget, EU funding for Ukraine must be shoe-horned into existing budget commitments. Its European Peace Facility, established in 2021, has allocated €5.6 billion to Ukraine, almost half the Facility's seven-year budget. Additional funding for the Facility has been caught up in wrangling between national governments about how much each government should contribute. It now has a commitment to give Ukraine €12.5 billion annually for four years. This is less than the EU spends on development aid for countries on other continents (Charlemagne, 2024; IfW, 2024).

When the Eurobarometer survey asks about EU policy towards Ukraine, a majority of respondents consistently favour giving it support; the size of the majority varies with the type of support (Figure 8.1). Humanitarian measures, which account for less than 5 per cent of the EU's aid to Ukraine, are overwhelmingly endorsed. Financial assistance and economic sanctions are approved by 72 per cent of respondents and three-fifths approve in principle supplying military equipment to Ukraine (Thomson et al., 2023). No question is asked about sending European troops to fight alongside Ukrainians because the EU has no armed force. A January 2024 survey in a dozen EU member states found that 41 per cent would like to see the EU push Ukraine towards negotiating a peace deal with Russia as against 31 per cent favouring support for Ukraine continuing until it had regained territories occupied by Russia (Krastev and Leonard, 2024: 8).

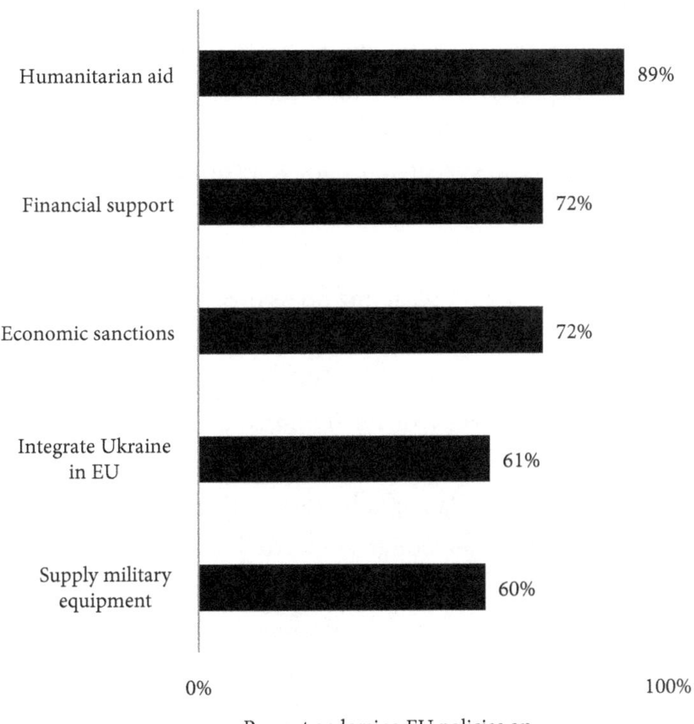

Figure 8.1 European support for assistance to Ukraine

Source: Standard Eurobarometer 100 survey in 27 states, 23 October–15 November 2023.

National governments turn to Washington. The government of each EU member state is responsible for the military defence of its country and free to join a military alliance of its choice. In response to the Soviet Union reducing East European countries to client states following the end of the Second World War, West European countries sought protection by joining NATO, a military alliance led by the United States. By the time Russia invaded Ukraine, twenty-two EU member states were NATO members.

The Russian violation of Ukraine's neutrality, which it intended to prevent NATO from placing arms at its borders, has had the opposite effect. The Finnish government concluded that the risk of Russia reacting against it joining NATO was much less than the risk of remaining neutral. Finland is now a NATO member. A Swedish diplomat described his country's decision to join NATO after the Russian invasion of Ukraine as 'the first radical shift in its basic security posture since Sweden adopted neutrality at the time of the Napoleonic wars' (Moody, 2023).

European public opinion strongly supports looking across the Atlantic for military security; the European Union is sidelined. When the European Security survey asked people where their country should turn for military allies, 64 per cent endorsed allying with NATO or with its hegemon, the United States (Figure 8.2). By contrast, only 10 per cent favoured looking to the European Union for help with defence and only one-quarter thought their country would be better off acting on its own when dealing with military threats.

The European desire to rely on NATO for defence requires the assent of the American government. Donald Trump's 2024 presidential campaign website has cryptically stated, 'We have to finish the process we began under my administration of fundamentally re-evaluating NATO's purpose and NATO's mission'. In response, Congress inserted in the 2024 National Defence Authorization Act a clause requiring a two-thirds vote of approval by the Senate to confirm American withdrawal from NATO.

If American aid for Ukraine was significantly reduced, a January 2024 survey in twelve countries found that only a fifth of respondents endorsed European governments filling the resulting gap in Ukraine's needs. A fifth endorsed keeping the existing level of aid unchanged, and one-third favoured following the American lead, limiting support and encouraging Ukraine to make a peace deal with Russia (Krastev and Leonard, 2024: 14).

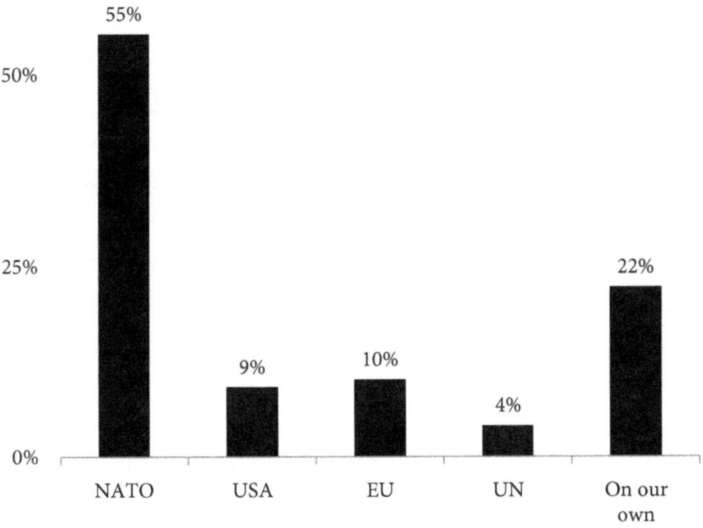

Figure 8.2 Ally best suited to help with military threats

Source: European Security Survey, December, 2022 in seven EU states plus United Kingdom. See Rose and Wessels, 2023.

The possibility of the United States becoming an unreliable defender has stimulated European security experts to think about creating a military force that is not dependent on the outcome of an American election. For the French government, which is one of Europe's two nuclear powers, this would be an opportunity to gain strategic autonomy from the United States. For the UK it offers the prospect of regaining a leadership role in Europe lost by leaving the EU. For Germany, it would mean abandoning the belief that it no longer needs an army strong enough to defend itself. For all European states, an end to outsourcing military defence to the United States would involve going without a united European force to deter Russia until 2030. In the words of a British minister of defence, this would be 'Europe's darkest hour' (Brown, 2024).

National interests differ. When European governments have co-operated to protect their security, this is due to similar calculations of national interest. When there are differences in national interests, the EU's requirement of super-majorities or unanimity for decisions gives every government the means to delay or frustrate cooperation in security.

National interests have resulted in the EU's effort to co-ordinate the efficient procurement of military equipment being met by national governments seeking exemptions to protect their own arms producers. National governments give greater priority to self-sufficiency in war materials than to the economic efficiency that could result from competitive bidding in a Single European Market. When the EU proposed allowing Ukraine to export grain to the EU to raise funds for its defence, five East European countries were exempted because they protested that this would hurt their own farmers' income. When the exemption expired in September 2023, Poland, Hungary and Slovakia re-imposed national bans on imports in defiance of EU rules.

Differences in the views of national governments have created crises and delays in EU funding for Ukraine that parallel the problems that the White House faces in seeking Ukraine aid from Congress. The EU's four-year €50 billion aid package was bogged down in negotiations for seven months by countries more concerned about the cost than Ukraine's urgent need for aid. Five EU national leaders from Germany, Denmark, the Czech Republic, Estonia and the Netherlands had to go so far as to publish a letter in the *Financial Times* addressed to their fellow member states (Scholz et al., 2024). They declared that the EU should maintain the supply of weapons and money as long as it takes to protect 'our common European security'.

The amount of money that national governments have allocated to support Ukraine reflects differences about the priority given spending on social policies and national security (IfW, 2024). When aid is evaluated as a percentage of a country's GDP, the five leading countries – Estonia, Lithuania, Estonia, Norway and Denmark – are countries too close to Russia for comfort. When aid is evaluated in terms of how much money is committed, only one country among the leaders, Germany, is a member of the European Union. The other countries giving large amounts of aid – the United States, the United Kingdom, Canada, Norway and Japan – are not in the EU.

Bibliography

Boyes, Roger, 2024. 'Another Big War in 2024 Will Test the West to Its Limits'. *The Times*, 6 January.

Brown, Larisa, 2024. 'Europe Acts over Fear US Will Block Aid to Ukraine'. *The Times*, 1 January.

Bureau of Political-Military Affairs, 2023. *US Security Cooperation with Ukraine*. Washington, DC: US Department of State.

Charlemagne, 2024. 'The Hour of Europe Chimes Again'. *The Economist*, 27 January.

Christiansen, Thomas, et al., 2000. 'Fuzzy Politics around Fuzzy Borders: The European Union's Near Abroad'. *Cooperation and Conflict*, 35, 4, 389–415.

Gstöl, Sieglinde and Schunz, Simon, eds., 2022. *The External Action of the European Union*. London: Bloomsbury Academic.

Hoffman, Elizabeth, Han, Jaehyun, and Vakharia, Shivani, 2023. 'The Past, Present, and Future of US Assistance to Ukraine'. Washington, DC: Center for Strategic and International Studies, September 26. www.csis.org/analysis/past-present-and-future-us-assistance-ukraine-deep-dive-data.

IfW, 2024. *Ukraine Support Tracker*. Kiel: Institut für Weltwirtschaft. www.ifw-kiel.de/topics/war-against-ukraine/ukraine-support-tracker/ consulted 20 February 2024.

Kaufmann, Sylvie, 2023. 'Europe Must Not Be Caught Short if Trump Wins Again'. *Financial Times*, 22 December.

Krastev, Ivan and Leonard, Mark, 2024. *Wars and Elections: How European Leaders Can Maintain Public Support for Ukraine*. London: European Council on Foreign Relations Policy Brief.

Levada Centre, 2024. 'Conflict with Ukraine'. https://www.levada.ru/en/2024/03/27/conflict-with-ukraine-estimates-of-the-end-of-2023-beginning-of-2024/.

Mills, Claire, 2024. *Sanctions against Russia*. London: House of Commons Research Briefing 9481.

Moody, Oliver, 2023. 'Russia, Gangs and Islamism Put End to Scandi Dream'. *The Times*, 7 November.

NATO, 2023. *Defence Expenditures of NATO Countries (2014–2023)*. Brussels: NATO.

NATO, 2024. *Relations with NATO*. Brussels: NATO, 7 March.

Pew Center, 2023. 'What Public Opinion Surveys Found in the First Year of the War in Ukraine'. Washington, DC: Pew Research Center. www.pewresearch.org/short-reads/2023/02/23/what-public-opinion-surveys-found-in-the-first-year-of-the-war-in-ukraine.

Pew Center, 2024. 'Survey 22–28 January'. https://twitter.com/pewresearch/status/1759732856245330206.

Politi, James and Fedor, Lauren, 2024. 'Candidates Offer Clashing Foreign Policy Visions'. *Financial Times*, 23 January.

Pukhov, Ruslan N., 2024. 'From Special to Military'. *Russia in Global Politics*, 22, 2, 112–26.

Rose, Richard and Wessels, Bernard, 2023. *Who Can Help Us with Threats to Our Security?* Berlin: Wissenschaftszentrum Berlin.

Sasse, Gwendolyn, 2023. *Russia's War against Ukraine.* Cambridge: Polity.

Scholz, Olaf, Frederiksen, Mette, Fiala, Petr, Kallas, Kaja and Rutte, Mark, 2024. 'All for a Collective Effort to Arm Ukraine for the Long Term'. *Financial Times*, 31 January.

Shevtsova, Lilia, 2020. 'Russia's Ukraine Obsession'. *Journal of Democracy,* 31, 1, 138–47.

Shuster, Simon, 2024. *The Showman.* London: William Collins.

Smeltz, Dina and El Baz, Lama, 2023. *American Public Support for Assistance to Ukraine Has Waned, but Still Considerable.* Chicago: Chicago Council on Global Affairs.

Snyder, Timothy, 2010. *Bloodlands: Europe between Hitler and Stalin.* New York: Basic Books.

Stebelsky, Ihor, 2009. 'Ethnic Self-Identification in Ukraine, 1989–2001: Why More Ukrainians and Fewer Russians?'. *Canadian Slavonic Papers,* 51, 1, 77–100. http://www.jstor.org/stable/40871355.

Steinhart, Erik C., 2015. *The Holocaust and the Germanization of Ukraine.* Cambridge: Cambridge University Press.

Szporluk, Roman, 2000. *Russia, Ukraine, and the Breakup of the Soviet Union.* Stanford: Hoover Institution Press.

Thomson, Catarina, Mader, Matthias, Münchow, Felix, Reifler, Jason and Schoen, Harald, 2023. 'European Public Opinion: United in Supporting Ukraine; Divided on Future of NATO'. *International Affairs*, 99, 6, 2485–500.

Whiteley, Paul, 2024. *Ukraine War: What the US Public Thinks about Giving Military and other Aid.* London: The Conversation. https://theconversation.com/ukraine-war-what-the-us-public-thinks-about-giving-military-and-other-aid-223064.

9

The future of European security

Security is a continuing responsibility of government, but the intensity of threats varies greatly over time. The Russian invasion of Ukraine has changed security from being a problem in the abstract to a problem near at hand. It was last at this point just after the end of the Second World War. However, within a decade the intensity of that threat subsided with the creation of NATO. The deterrence effect of the American commitment to European security outlasted the Soviet Union. Vladimir Putin has made security once again a top European concern by Russia's invasion of Ukraine.

Wars are short in terms of time, but they have long-term consequences. As fighting in Ukraine continues there are three contrasting scenarios about how the war might end. The first is that the conflict turns into a stalemate with Russian troops unable to gain more Ukraine territory but strong enough on the defensive to keep control of the territory Russia now holds. An armistice is agreed which is similar to that in Korea in 1953: the fighting stops and Russia continues to occupy Ukrainian territory. To deal with the risk of Russia re-launching the war, Ukraine would seek a long-term guarantee of military assistance, preferably from NATO, to replace the ad hoc assistance that the United States and Europe now provide.

A second possible outcome is that Russia forces Ukraine to surrender by occupying Kyiv and setting up a puppet government favourable to Moscow. This would create a Cold War boundary, in which NATO would respect Russia's territorial conquest and re-arm heavily to defend its current member states. Putin might test the resolve of the United States and Europe to start a Third World War by occupying Narva, a predominantly Russian-speaking city on the Estonian side of its international border with Russia. A third alternative is that Ukraine regains territory that Russia has occupied since 2014. If this were to happen, it would want Western aid to fortify its border against a renewed attack, and NATO countries would still need to maintain a significant military presence along their eastern borders to deter Russia.

When the fighting stops in Ukraine is not now known, but there are already important knowns about challenges arising once the conflict ends. First of all, Russia will remain a threat to European security for the indefinite future. This will encourage Western allies to give some form of guarantee of Ukraine's security to deter repeated aggression. Secondly, the cost of reconstructing a country that has been a battlefield for years will be greater than Ukraine can meet on its own. It will look to its wartime allies for continued assistance. Thirdly, having accepted Ukraine and western Balkan countries as candidates for joining an enlarged European Union, the EU will be challenged to reform its own institutions to absorb many more diverse states. Moreover, insofar as electoral politics makes the United States a less reliable ally, European governments will need to create a European security institution as a backup for America's role in protecting the security of North Atlantic Europe.

Deterring further Russian aggression?

Whether the war in Ukraine ends with one side victorious and the other defeated or both sides making heavily discounted claims to victory, it will usher in another period of cold war. Russia will still control parts of Georgia and Moldova and the government of Belarus, with its long border with Europe, will remain a satellite of Moscow. In the Baltic, Russian troops border five NATO and EU members: Estonia, Latvia, Lithuania, Poland and Finland. The former president of Russia Dmitry Medvedev has threatened the death of Polish statehood if it continues to support Ukraine. There is thus a need for governments to maintain sufficient armed forces to deter aggression or, failing that, to repel it on the grounds of the Roman motto, *Si vis pacem, para bellum* (If you want peace, prepare for war).

What Ukraine wants: Allies guaranteeing security. Even if the war ends with Ukraine regaining all the territory that Russia has occupied, this does not guarantee its security from another invasion. It will want a strong guarantee of its security by the United States to deter Russia from future aggression. Unlike the costs the United States has met to support Ukraine fighting a proxy war, a security guarantee need not cost a massive amount of money. However, it carries the risk that if deterrence fails and Russia again attacks, the United States is then committed to come to Ukraine's aid in a war with Russia.

The deterrence effect would be greatest if Ukraine became a NATO member. Ukraine formally submitted an application to join NATO in September 2022. Nine ex-communist NATO member states promptly supported it joining the alliance at some future date. However, there are conditions that would have to be met before Ukraine could become a NATO member. First of all, Russia should not be in so strong a military position when the fighting ends that it can dictate a clause in the armistice treaty forbidding Ukraine gaining NATO membership. Secondly, Ukraine would have to turn the self-defence force it has rapidly mobilized into a professional force that can be integrated into NATO's professional multi-national forces. Thirdly, member states must give unanimous approval to a candidate becoming a new member. Unanimity cannot be taken for granted. NATO membership would require approval not only by the White House but also by the Pentagon accepting its military implications and by the Senate ratifying the new treaty commitment. It could also be vetoed by a pro-Putin government of a country that is now a NATO member.

Deterrence may also be achieved by a credible statement of American intent to act in defence of Ukraine in the event of aggression. Credibility does not require a treaty. The Truman Doctrine deterring Russia from taking over two Eastern Mediterranean countries was set out in a presidential speech to Congress declaring it was in the American interest to provide them with military assistance. A strong presidential statement endorsed by a Congressional resolution would be an *a priori* warning to Russia of the risk it would face in violating an armistice.

Unlike a treaty commitment, which binds the government of the United States, a presidential commitment is vulnerable to change after an election. For that reason, Ukraine would also want to strengthen its capacity for defending itself on its own. This would require a guarantee to be supplemented by short-term aid from the United States and NATO to train a large defence force and to produce its own military equipment. It would also want support, whether bilateral or collective, from governments in Europe.

What Washington wants: An end to NATO free-riding. The US government has repeatedly made clear that it wants NATO members to share the cost of collective defence according to their means. There are differences between states of more than twenty times in the total sum each spends, reflecting in part differences in the their economic size and in part differences in their political will. Thus, the American government meets more than half the total cost of Europe's military defence (cf. NATO, 2023; Samuel, 2023). This reflects the great majority of European governments giving a lower priority to military security than does the United States.

The low level of European spending on defence has led to a widespread sense in Washington that European countries are free-riding for their defence on the backs of the American taxpayer. Donald Trump's vice-presidential candidate, J. D. Vance (2024), estimates that if European countries had maintained Cold War levels of defence spending rather than cutting them, they would have spent an additional $8.6 trillion in three decades. He describes, 'the cash the continent hasn't spent should be seen for what it really is: a tax on the American people'.

The target for a member state's defence expenditure is 2 per cent of its gross domestic product. During the Cold War many major European governments spent above this figure. The break-up of the Soviet Union led European governments to feel more secure and reduced military spending substantially. When Russia seized control of Crimea in 2014, the United States was spending 3.7 per cent of its GDP on defence. Only the UK and Greece also met the 2 per cent spending target; the average European member of NATO was spending 1.4 per cent of its GDP on defence. After prodding by the Trump administration, by 2021 eight NATO members besides the United States reported spending at least 2 per cent of GDP on defence. While the average expenditure by a European government had risen, it was still less than half the effort that the US government was making to deter aggression.

The invasion of Ukraine has prompted a significant boost in military expenditure on both sides of the Atlantic. Between 2014 and 2023 total NATO expenditure rose by more than one-fifth at constant prices, and in percentage terms it rose more in Europe. A history of Russian domination has led Poland to double its military spending to an even larger share of GDP than that of the United States. A total of eleven European countries, eight of which bordered the territory of the former Soviet Union, now meet the NATO expenditure standard. However, because these states are less populous and have a lower GDP, collectively they account for less than a tenth of total NATO spending. Of the three largest European Union countries, none met the target. France spent 1.9 per cent of its GDP on defence, Germany has committed to spending at least 1.5 per cent and Italy 1.4 per cent of its GDP.

Under pressure from Washington as well as the proxy war in Ukraine, a substantial majority of European countries have pledged to spend at least 2 per cent of their GDP on defence. However, there are doubts about how soon or whether all countries can actually spend the money committed in their budgets. Given a history of limited demand for military equipment in the past, defence industries in countries such as Germany are having difficulty in meeting the national demand for such military necessities as ammunition and missiles. Lengthy bureaucratic procedures controlling the procurement of military equipment hold back production too.

In every NATO country claims for increased military spending compete with claims to increase spending on social programmes to take care of an ageing population, technology investment to maintain economic competitiveness and subsidies to reduce the impact of the rising cost of living. If Germany were to spend 2 per cent of its GDP on defence, it would have to reduce spending on social programmes by tens of billions of euros. In the words of a senior NATO official, 'Leaders have signed up to a generational shift in defence policy. I do wonder if they fully understand or have told their finance ministers' (Major and Moelling, 2023; Rathbone, 2023).

The American federal government faces political constraints on its budget too, even though social programmes account for a lower but growing share of the federal budget than in Europe. Before Russia invaded Ukraine, there was resistance in Congress to raising taxes or increasing debt-financed spending. Putting a cap on foreign aid has a political justification too. It gives American politicians a club that can be used to threaten European governments with the loss of American protection if they do not spend more for their own security. Moreover, regardless of the occupant of the White House, the United States is a global power facing multiple security threats across continents. Thus, there is competition for funding European security from threats in the Near East and in the China seas. Ukraine's president has pointedly noted that the United

States has been readier to provide high-powered weapons to Israel in its war against Palestine terrorist than to Ukraine.

What Europe needs: A reliable security force. Most European countries are too small to defend themselves against Russia. Since Napoleon's time, they have sought security by being part of an alliance. Being allied to the United States through NATO leverages a country's power many times over. For the immediate future, European governments have no alternative but to rely on Article 5 of the NATO Treaty, which commits the United States to come to their military aid in the event of a Russian invasion. However, American political developments have reduced the reliability of this commitment. This has prompted leaders of major European governments to consider security options that do not depend on decisions taken in Washington.

While the European Union has the soft power of diplomacy to deal with foreign affairs, hard power is required to deal with military aggression, and the EU lacks a military force. France, under presidents from Charles de Gaulle to Emmanuel Macron, has proposed creating a European defence force that could act independently of NATO. However, in the past many European countries have not wanted to do anything that would reduce the commitment of a Washington-led alliance mobilizing massive American firepower (cf. Anderson, 2022: 83; Hofmann, 2013; Rynning, 2024).

Political developments in Washington and Moscow have prompted a reconsideration of forming a European force with the capability to deter Russian aggression. The UK and France each has its own nuclear weapons, the ultimate deterrent against a direct attack by an enemy. However, Russia has neither the interest nor the capability of using land troops to invade either country. The most likely form of Russian aggression is a land invasion of a country on its border. For either Britain or France to use nuclear weapons in response to Moscow's troops invading an East European country would be grossly disproportionate and invite Russia's nuclear retaliation. Their value is greatest in backing up a European army fighting a land war against invading Russian troops.

The German federal government has always looked to Washington for its military security and assumed economic interdependence would give the Russian state an incentive to maintain a peaceful relationship. Russia's weaponization of its supply of vital energy to Germany has shattered that belief.

While the German government has recognized a turning point in European security, it also need what its defence minister has called a *Mentalitätswechsel*, a change in attitudes towards military defence so that it is capable of fighting a war (*Tagesschau*, 2023).

A by-product of the war in Ukraine is that the accession of Finland and Sweden to NATO has made the Baltic region on Russia's northern flank a NATO lake. With the exception of Russia, all countries bordering the Baltic Sea now belong to NATO and six have land borders directly vulnerable to invasion by Russia. The countries have shown the strength of their political will by maintaining well equipped armed forces, backed up by forms of conscription that provide a ready reserve for use in an emergency. Moreover, they are ready to collaborate for their mutual defence through a collective force that could be quickly mobilized to resist Russian invasion without reliance on American forces. Britain's readiness to support the group gives it an ally with a nuclear force (see Chapter 10). However, there is no collective mobilization of NATO members on Russia's southern flank and borders with Belarus and Ukraine. Some governments do not want to regard Russia as a threat requiring increased military security or are even pro-Putin, as is the case of Viktor Orban's government in Hungary.

The immediate problem facing Europeans is that Russia is now on a war footing, with a large and battle-hardened army, ample military equipment and the political will to use force to take control of territory in its near abroad. By contrast, European governments are just starting to increase their military strength, a process that will take years, and to increase cross-national military cooperation. Some countries have not yet seen the need to do so. As long as this is the case, European countries must rely on the United States for the military force to deter Russian aggression.

Who pays to rebuild Ukraine?

A big cost. The resources needed for rebuilding Ukraine are massive, whatever currency is used to calculate the total. Moreover, the costs are growing every day that the war continues. At the individual level, the war has injured hundreds of thousands of civilians as well as soldiers. Russian drones and shelling have damaged 10 per cent of the country's housing in the first two years of the war. While owners of single-family homes may do a lot of repairs themselves, the large number of dwellers in multi-storey apartment blocks will need state-financed reconstruction for their housing to be restored to what it was before the war. In agriculture there is a need in battleground regions to check the ground for land mines that have been planted in great profusion and to clear fields of the wreckage left by armies on both sides.

There is nationwide damage to roads, bridges, energy sources and urban buildings due to attack by drones. Up to a point, repairs and replacement may upgrade infrastructure that is a legacy of shoddy Soviet workmanship. There will also be a positive gain rebuilding and updating factories and service facilities that have been damaged. Once economic infrastructure is repaired, there is a clear pathway to the recovery of the country's GDP.

The cost of making good the damage to Ukraine has been estimated as $486 billion at the beginning of 2024, equivalent to almost three times Ukraine's GDP. The cost continues to rise as the war lengthens and the extent of damage is such that it will take up to a decade to complete reconstruction. Whatever the ultimate cost of rebuilding Ukraine, it will be much more than what can be raised within the country.

What Ukraine can contribute. Ukraine's GDP per capita is low. After adjusting for purchasing power parity it is only two-fifths that of Russia, one-third that of Poland and lower still by comparison with the average European Union country. Nonetheless, Ukraine is a country well endowed with natural resources. More than 55 per cent of its large territory is suitable for agriculture. It is the world's largest producer of sunflower products and one of the world's largest producers of corn, wheat and barley. Agricultural exports from its Black Sea ports to the EU and developing countries accounted for more than two-fifths of Ukraine's total exports the year before Russia invaded, and the disruption of its agricultural exports has created global shortages feeding higher prices. The country has substantial deposits of iron ore and coal to support industrial production and significant, though not self-sufficient, energy resources and nuclear power. Heavy industrial goods tend to be produced in eastern Ukraine.

Ukraine's human capital is at European standards. The Soviet era gave a high priority to mass education at the primary and secondary level, and universities were founded as early as the sixteenth century. Ukraine has hundreds of institutions granting degrees and before the war about 1.5 million young people were enrolled in tertiary education. A total of 51 per cent of men and 65 per cent of women had a tertiary-level qualification in 2021. This was the highest proportion of qualified workers of any country covered by the EU's European Neighbourhood Policy.

Ukraine's political institutions are a long-established liability. In Soviet times corruption was institutionalized as a way of getting things done. Independence created a group of wealthy oligarchs with political connections in Moscow as well as Kyiv. Competitive elections have produced unstable governments alternating between pro-Moscow and pro-Brussels parties. The Russian invasion has produced a government of national unity purged of supporters with ties to Moscow. However, it has not reduced corruption to European levels. The imposition of martial law during the war has put a stop to party politics but not corruption. It leaves open the extent to which Ukrainian politicians will default to their pre-war practices or compete in post-war elections on their ability to manage the reconstruction of their society. The capacity of a post-war Ukrainian government to manage rebuilding is problematic.

Europe gets the bill. While American politics is full of uncertainties, one thing is certain: the rebuilding of Ukraine will not be financed by the US government. Financing Ukraine's proxy war with Russia has reduced the political capital needed to send money to Ukraine, and the first post-war priority will be to contribute to Ukraine's military defence. This will leave Europeans with the challenge of financing the rebuilding of the country.

Given the cost of Ukraine's reconstruction, money must come from a variety of sources, each making decisions in keeping with their own rules and priorities. Ukrainian public and private sector institutions likewise come in different shapes and sizes. In economic theory there is an ideal equilibrium between the supply and demand for reconstruction funds. In practice, there are multiple equilibrium points. An optimistic possibility is that a large amount of international finance results in Ukraine's economy enjoying a period of rapid economic growth that can more than repay the cost of reconstruction. A pessimistic scenario is that there is a low-level equilibrium trap in which reconstruction funds are limited and spent in inefficient ways doing little to produce the economic growth that Ukraine needs to reach the standard of a European economy.

The European Union's current budget commitments, which are fixed until 2027, were set before Russia attacked Ukraine and leave little scope for outlays of the size required to rebuild Ukraine. Total EU aid appears large only because a number of member states prefer to channel their support through the EU. However, it is much less than the total amount that Ukraine requires for its rebuilding.

To rebuild war damage, Ukraine may draw upon a wide range of inter-governmental financial institutions. The European Investment Bank is the lending arm of the European Union. It offers loans, guarantees, equity investments and advisory services to promote development. In the first year of the war it allocated €1.7 billion to repair infrastructure and a credit of €4 billion to support Ukrainian refugees in member states. Ukraine is a member of the European Bank for Reconstruction and Development (EBRD), established in 1991 to assist ex-communist countries in reconstructing their economies. While the EBRD cannot provide support to government, it can provide aid to state-owned utilities supplying electricity and rail transport. The World Bank has co-ordinated programmes to pay public employees and ensure the continued delivery of essential services such as health care and education. The European Central Bank website describes it as indirectly supporting Ukraine through financial sanctions on Russia and measures to cushion the financial impact of the war on countries in the eurozone.

More than three dozen countries are providing direct bilateral economic assistance to Ukraine rather than making contributions through Brussels (IfW Kiel, 2023). Norway, a non-EU member state, is contributing more money than any EU member state except Germany. Among the ten countries contributing the biggest share of their GDP to assist Ukraine, six were formerly subject to Soviet control. More than a dozen countries outside the European Union are already making bilateral commitments of money to Ukraine. The group includes five Anglo-American countries and Japan, Korea and India. Before the war started, China became a larger trading partner with Ukraine than any single European country and President Zelensky has endorsed the idea of Ukraine offering China a 'bridge to Europe' (*The Economist*, 2023).

Banks and investment firms are ready to purchase bonds and make loans to finance Ukraine's rebuilding as long as there is a sufficient premium to send money to a country that is much less secure than the average European state. This requires a high interest rate and an institution to guarantee lenders they will be paid in the event a Ukrainian borrower defaults. While the first condition adds to the cost of private finance, the second need not if loans are properly evaluated and monitored to guard against mismanagement and default. Multi-national firms are prepared to undertake projects to rebuild damaged infrastructure as long as they are guaranteed they will be paid, for example, if contracts for work in Ukraine are made with a non-Ukraine funder. Given that wages for skilled labour are low by EU standards, Ukraine can have a significant competitive advantage if it is admitted to the Single European Market.

Doing nothing or just enough to appear helpful is always an option. However, this would leave the wreckage of a large, resource-rich country on the border of EU member states with uncertain security implications. Moreover, Ukraine would be vulnerable to attempts by Moscow to re-establish its influence there by the usual KGB methods. In the words of the president of the EBRD, 'The cost of not supporting Ukraine is going to be higher than supporting it' (Hall, 2023).

Is the EU fit to admit Ukraine?

In 2016 the president of the European Commission, Jean-Claude Juncker, said that it would take twenty to twenty-five years for Ukraine to meet the requirements needed to become a member of the European Union. However, the war in Ukraine has radically shortened that time scale. Weeks after Russian forces invaded, Ukraine formally applied for EU membership. The German foreign minister has described enlarging the EU to include Ukraine, Moldova, Georgia and western Balkan countries as a 'geopolitical necessity' to protect the EU's eastern borders (Baerbock, 2023). In December 2023 the European Council approved starting the process of evaluating the suitability of Ukraine and Moldova for membership. The president of the Council set 2030 as the date when the EU should be ready for its most important enlargement in a quarter-century.

When announcing that the EU was ready to consider the admission of Ukraine, the European Council President Charles Michel declared, 'We need to reflect on the EU's capacity to act and to achieve its objectives' (Waterfield, 2023). The EU's problems in managing its affairs were well known before the Russian invasion of Ukraine. Many solutions are also well known, some of which take into account the obstacles to resolving difficulties and some do not. If enlargement is not to make the EU weaker rather than stronger, it must face up to the long-postponed need to reform its economic and political institutions.

The cash cost. Admitting Ukraine will impose a substantial economic cost on the EU's annual budget. Before the war, Ukraine's GDP per capita was only one-quarter the average of EU member states. This will qualify it to receive EU agricultural subsidies and social cohesion funds, which account for three-fifths of the EU's total expenditure. In both cases Ukraine's total claim on the EU budget will be large, as its population is four times that of the EU's median member state and its agricultural land is similar in size to the whole of France.

Ukraine's claim on the EU budget can be estimated by applying existing EU rules to Ukraine's economy the year before Russia invaded. On that basis, Ukraine would receive about €18 billion annually from the EU's budget (Emerson, 2023). This is approximately one-tenth of total EU expenditure and almost double what the EU has been giving Poland, which has a population similar to Ukraine. It is also five times the total benefit that would be paid to six western Balkan states with small populations if they were simultaneously admitted to the EU. Paying agricultural subsidies on a per hectare basis would benefit Ukrainians owning mega-farms, a legacy of the Soviet era.

Paying subsidies to Ukraine would require increased national contributions by many existing member states, thereby mobilizing opposition from fiscally conservative governments and anti-EU populists. Alternatively, the money could be found by reducing payments that many member states currently receive from the EU's agricultural and social cohesion policies. Better-off countries such as France and Germany would lose up to a fifth of the money that these policies pay them.

All estimates of the financial cost of admitting Ukraine as an EU member are based on the assumption that 'all other conditions remain equal'. This is emphatically not the case for Ukraine once the fighting stops. Years of fighting are likely to shrink the size of its economy, thereby qualifying it for more money under existing rules. The length of time it will take a reconstructed

Ukrainian economy to catch up with the least well-off EU members is a major unknown. One thing is certain: the loss of hundreds of millions in EU grants by every existing member state would create an immediate economic problem for hard-pressed national ministers of finance. It would also encourage national governments to put Ukraine's request for EU admission on indefinite hold. If this crisis in funding led to a major reform of existing EU spending priorities, which have been urged for decades, this would reduce Ukraine's claims on the EU's purse but also reduce Ukraine's funds for development.

Political frictions. The European Union's political criteria for evaluating candidates for accession include having democratic institutions, a market economy and respect for the rule of law and the rights of minorities. Evaluating how much Ukraine's government can or will do to put an end to pre-war practices that would disqualify it from EU membership is difficult. Admission to the European Union would also require major political changes in West Balkan states. The EU has found from experience with Bulgaria and Romania that admitting a country in hopes that membership will raise a country's governing standards has not worked.

Enlarging the EU by the admission of up to eight more countries would give its collegial institutions almost six times as many members as they were originally meant to serve. This would place pressure on existing institutions to reform decision-making institutions already under strain. Arguably, reforms would produce a collective benefit for member states old and new. However, the process of overcoming existing obstacles to change would create political frictions.

Decision-making today requires unanimity on major issues or a super-majority including smaller and populous states. The effect of a high hurdle of approval is to encourage negotiation and compromise in order to arrive at a consensus in which all or nearly all countries secure most of their goals, if only partially. More than four-fifths of decisions are reached in this way. However, major security policies tend to require unanimous approval. As a member state, Ukraine could threaten to use its veto in order to gain benefits arising from its experience of war. Admitting West Balkan countries would substantially increase the number of small countries needing conciliation before a consensus could be reached.

Each member state can currently nominate a politician to serve as the head of a directorate-general in the European Commission, a position analogous to being a cabinet minister in a national government. Even though commissioners are meant to advance the EU's supra-national goals, they also provide their national government with access to inside knowledge of what the Commission is considering. Adding all applicants for membership would result in almost one-quarter of the Commission's departments being headed by EU novices and create an unwieldy Commission fragmented into almost three dozen directorates. The number of directorates could be reduced by halving their number and giving each two commissioners. One could be a lead commissioner and the other a deputy and the lead position rotating between the two commissioners at the halfway mark of their five-year term (Franco-German Working Group, 2023: 20).

Can crisis force change? Theories of the European Union emphasize that a crisis can force positive change. The fall of the Berlin Wall is an example of a major crisis that led to new EU treaties expanding its powers and doubling its membership to include new East European members from Finland to the Black Sea. The pressure for change was used by the then president of the European Commission, Jacques Delors, to accelerate moves towards European integration and accepted by French and German leaders as a means of preventing German unification from creating a super-size state that could pursue its national interest unchecked.

The Russian invasion of Ukraine created an immediate military crisis: the consequences of an end to fighting are long-lasting. The economic costs of rebuilding Ukraine involve hundreds of billions of dollars, but are marginal in an EU that has a gross domestic product of more than €15 trillion annually. They are also manageable because the cost will be spread over a decade or more. The pressure to cut EU subsidies for agriculture and social cohesion can arguably be seen as leading to a more efficient Single European Market. Given Ukraine's substantial natural resources and human capital, spending money to reconstruct its war-damaged economy has the potential to offer a long-term return on investment. Poland, which has a similar population and history of a communist economy, now has a larger GDP than all but five of the EU's twenty-seven economies. Once the fighting stops, Ukraine must reform its governance to meet EU entrance requirements. Until it does so, it remains in the category of Soviet successor states. In parallel, the EU must reform its institutions. Insofar as reforms make the European Union more efficient and effective, this will be worthwhile in itself and facilitate further steps towards European integration. However, getting twenty-seven national governments to give unanimous approval of a reform treaty is time-consuming.

Washington's challenge to European security

The war in Ukraine has forced European governments to pay much more attention to military security. The rate at which Ukraine is burning ammunition in self-defence has revealed that European countries lack the capacity to produce sufficient armaments for their own security. To meet Ukraine's immediate need for equipment to fight a proxy war, European governments are buying military equipment from the United States, the Republic of Korea and Israel. Nor is there a European defence force, operating within or outside NATO, to take action independently of the United States. For the foreseeable future, European governments have no desire to give up their reliance on the American commitment to defend Europe. However, its maintenance depends on Washington politics.

A bipartisan commitment linking the defence of European security with American national security long enabled European governments to rely on the United States for its own security. That commitment no longer exists. The president faces not only enemies abroad but also enemies at home. There is no longer a Washington consensus about how or whether the United States should maintain its NATO commitment to defend Europe. Moreover, there are divisions about security policies within each party. Democrats tend to support President Biden's policy but divisions have opened up within the party about how Israel has responded to the terrorist attack of Hamas. Republicans are divided between those who endorse maintaining America as the hegemonic leader of NATO coalition deterring Russia, advocates of giving greater priority to deterring Chinese power in Asia and isolationists who see immigration from Latin America as the priority threat (*The Economist*, 2024).

Biennial elections can institutionalize partisan divisions about security policy by placing control of one or both houses of Congress in the hands of the party in opposition to the White House. This happened in November 2022, when the Republican Party gained a majority in the House of Representatives, which has a major influence on the federal budget. This created major difficulties for President Biden; it also led to a four-month delay in authorizing a $67 billion appropriation to support Ukraine. Kamala Harris describes commitment to European security as part of a global policy in America's national interest.

A victory for Donald Trump in the November 2024 presidential election would face Europeans with uncertainty about their own security. Trump does not want the United States to withdraw from foreign affairs. He is a unilateralist, believing that with himself as president America can force other countries to do what he wants, for example, even claiming he could settle the war in Ukraine in a day (Belin, Ruge and Shapiro, 2023). What Trump wants is less clear in terms of policy than it is in personal terms. He wants to make himself appear powerful by dominating other politicians and countries. In the view of a Republican think-tank expert:

> No one knows what a Trump presidency would mean for foreign policy because Donald Trump has no actual vision, no guiding principles. It would depend on the deal, on the moment, on who insulted him last, and on the state. Certainly the 'establishment' is out. Whom does that leave? No one has a clue.
>
> (Politi, Fedor and Foy, 2024)

European governments wanting to maintain America's commitment to their defence can respond to a Trump victory by giving him what he wants: an end to what he describes as European free-riding on American tax-payers by spending at least 2 per cent of their gross domestic product on defence. Up to a point, this does not create a major political problem for European governments that have been falling short of this target, since they now have pledged to do so. While countries such as Germany face obstacles in boosting expenditure rapidly, the process could be accelerated by buying American military equipment. If European governments are prepared to face down domestic critics by challenging them to come up with a viable military alternative, then Trump can claim public credit and move on to whatever issue he fancies.

The known unknown is whether there is the political will among Europe's governments to increase their collective security. National governments closest to Russia in Eastern and Northern Europe have taken steps to strengthen their defence; none is large enough to deter Russian aggression on its own. The European Union has substantial power over a giant economy, but it is a military pygmy because it does not have the authority to maintain a European army. Given such obstacles, the default position is that the EU will continue making ad hoc arrangements with member states to support Ukraine, while member states will not agree to a new treaty that gives the EU the power to raise a European army that was vetoed by the French National Assembly in 1954. This falls short of the ebullient confidence of the president of the European Commission, Ursula von der Leyen: 'Europe is about making the impossible possible' (Fleming and Foy, 2023). It also leaves it up to the Kremlin to decide whether the uncertainties about the White House commitment to send troops to defend Europe are sufficiently strong to deter another Russian aggression.

Bibliography

Anderson, Stephanie, 2022. 'The EU's Security and Defense Policy a Decade after Lisbon'. In Federica Bindi, ed., *The Foreign Policy of the European Union*. Washington, DC: Brookings Institution, 3rd edition, 72–85.

Baerbock, Annalena, 2023. 'Foreign Minister Baerbock's Speech at the Conference on Europe in Berlin'. 2 November. www.auswaertiges-amt.de/en/newsroom/news/-/2629342.

Belin, Celia, Ruge, Magda and Shapiro, Jeremy, 2023. *Brace Yourself: How the 2024 US President Election Could Affect Europe*. London: European Council on Foreign Relations Policy Brief.

Economist, The, 2023. 'Eyeing Russia's Backyard'. 9 December.

Economist, The, 2024. 'Donald Trump's Foreign Policy'. 30 March.

Emerson, Michael, 2023. *The Potential Impact of Ukrainian Accession on the EU's Budget and the Importance of Control Valves*. Brussels: Centre for European Policy Studies.

European Commission, 2022. *On the Defence Investment Gaps: Analysis and Way Forward*. Brussels: Joint Communication JOIN (2022) 24 final.

Fleming, Sam and Foy, Henry, 2023. 'The Vast Consequences of Ukraine Joining the EU'. *Financial Times*, 7 August.

Franco-German Working Group, 2023. *Sailing on High Seas*. Paris and Berlin: Report of the Franco-German Working Group on EU Institutional Reform.

Hall, Ben, 2023. 'Reconstruction Bank to Double Kyiv Loans'. *Financial Times*, 20 December.

Hofmann, Stephanie C., 2013. *European Security in NATO's Shadow*. Cambridge: Cambridge University Press.

House of Commons, 2023. *UK Defence and the Indo-Pacific*. London: House of Commons Defence Committee, 11th Report of Session 2022–23.

IfW Kiel (Institut für Weltwirtschaft), 2023. Kiel, Germany. https://www.ifw-kiel.de/publications/news/ukraine-support-tracker.

Major, Claudia and Moelling, Christian, 2023. 'No Time to Lose'. *International Politik Quarterly*, 5 April. https://ip-quarterly.com/en/no-time-lose-how-germanys-zeitenwende-defense-can-succeed.

NATO, 2023. *Defence Expenditure of NATO Countries (2014–2023)*. Brussels: NATO.

OECD, 2009. *Explorations in OEEC History*. Paris: OECD Publishing. doi.org/10.1787/9789264067974-en.

Politi, James, Fedor, Lauren and Foy, Henry, 2024. 'Donald Trump Says Russia Can do What It Wants to Nato Allies Who Pay Too Little'. *Financial Times*, February 11.

Rathbone, John Paul, 2023. 'West Braced for Huge Costs after Loss of Peace Dividend'. *Financial Times*, September 13.

Rynning, Sten, 2024. *NATO: From Cold War to Ukraine*. New Haven: Yale University Press.

Samuel, Julia, 2023. 'Europe's Weak Defences Risk a Russian Attack'. *The Times*, 7 December.

Tagesschau, 2023. 'Interview with Boris Pistorius'. 12 November. www.tagesschau.de/inland/innenpolitik/pistorius-bundeswehr-114.html.

Vance, J. D., 2024. 'Europe Must Stand on Its Own Two Feet on Defence'. *Financial Times*, 20 February.

Waterfield, Bruno, 2023. 'Brussels Paves Way for Ukraine to Join European Union'. *The Times*, 9 November.

World Bank, 2024. *Third Rapid Damage and Needs Assessment: February 2022–December 2023*. Washington, DC: World Bank Group.

10

Where does Britain fit in?

At the start of the twentieth century the British government tried to maintain European security by being part of a balance of power. Two groups of countries formed opposing military alliances: the Central Powers, led by Germany and Austro-Hungary, and the Triple Entente, consisting of France, Russia and the UK. Instead of deterring war, the result was the outbreak of the First World War, when Austro-Hungary attacked an ally of Russia. In the 1930s Britain and France sought to balance the military threat of Nazi Germany by conceding Hitler's demands for strategic territories. Instead of being satisfied, Hitler formed an alliance with the Soviet Union that started the Second World War. In both cases the balance was only tipped in favour of the British side by the entry of the United States. Shortly after the end of the Second World War, the chief scientific advisor on British defence cautioned, 'We are not a Great Power and never will be again. We are a great nation, but if we continue to behave like a Great Power, we shall soon cease to be a great nation' (Quoted in Gowing, 1974: 229).

The maintenance of a cold peace in Europe by a balance of two non-European superpowers, the United States and Russia, has left Britain's leaders searching for a way to fit into this new global system. Winston Churchill proclaimed in a 1948 speech that Britain linked three majestic circles – the Empire and Commonwealth, the English-speaking world and a United Europe – that no force could challenge. Half a century later Tony Blair (1998: 18) declared that Britain had a global role unchanged since Churchill's day: 'strong partnerships with the EU, the US and in Asia'. Boris Johnson, in his first major speech as foreign secretary after the 2016 Brexit referendum, proclaimed a role for 'a global Britain running a global foreign policy'. An Anglophile advisor to

American presidents saw things differently. In 1962 Dean Acheson declared, 'Britain has lost an Empire and not yet found a role'. The question still lacks a realistic answer.

Although the rhetorical vision of Britain's global role has been effective as a domestic foreign policy, it has failed to impress foreigners. This chapter analyses what happens when British policymakers try to put their rhetoric into practice by finding a place for Britain in an insecure world. The next section describes how Britain's special relationship with the United States has shifted from an unequal partnership with common goals to a transactional relationship in the perspective of the White House while remaining a rhetorical bond in Downing Street. The English Channel has always been a mental as well as physical barrier to ties with Europe. Brexit has changed Britain's role from that of awkward partner in EU decision-making to a taker of EU economic decisions in which it has no say. The Russian invasion of Ukraine has created a global community of nations sharing a common interest in deterring Russian aggression and Britain has taken a political lead in Europe in offering support for Ukraine. However, the war has also revealed the limit on the military resources that Britain can mobilize on its own to stop aggression.

An asymmetrical relationship with the United States

The relationship between the United Kingdom and the United States has always been based on different perceptions. Until the Second World War broke out, the tradition of America's war of independence and Britain's global Empire kept relations distant. Britain's leaders were prepared to marry American women for the wealth they brought but not to see the United States as an ally adding weight to a European balance of power. This was radically transformed by Nazi Germany's attempt to conquer Britain and then by Hitler's unilateral declaration of war on the United States on the day that the United States was declaring war on Japan. This created a partnership with a shared interest in defeating Nazi Germany with an American general, Dwight D. Eisenhower, commanding joint military forces. The founding of NATO institutionalized American dominance in defence with the UK the principal trusted ally. Harold Macmillan's view of the special relationship forged in war was 'These

Americans represent the new Roman empire and we Britons, like the Greeks of old, must teach them how to make it go' (Ashton, 2005).

An unequal partnership. During the 1930s the United States maintained a policy of neutrality towards European disputes and was ready to defend its economic interests at Europe's expense. With the fall of France imminent in 1940, President Franklin D. Roosevelt delivered a fireside radio address declaring that it was in America's national interest to take heed of German aggression and launched a major rearmament programme. Thus, when Winston Churchill implored Roosevelt to send military supplies, arms were at hand that could be shipped Britain under a notional lend-lease arrangement. Anglo-American forces began joint military operations in North Africa in 1942 that continued until V-E Day.

Since the end of the Second World War, security cooperation has been strong, based on shared perceptions of specific military threats. Anglo-American cooperation on intelligence has developed into Five Eyes, a network of British, American, Canadian, Australian and New Zealand intelligence agencies that share information (Smith, 2022). The UK maintains a nuclear-armed fleet of submarines to deter any potential aggressor, but its nuclear weapons system depends on American supplies and technology. Since Britain has maintained a relatively stronger military force than other NATO members, there has been cooperation in field operations, sometimes successfully and sometimes not. It started with British troops joining the United States in Korea in 1950, in 2003 British troops joined the United States in invading Iraq, and in 2024 a British destroyer joined the American navy in fighting non-state Houthis shelling merchant ships in the Red Sea.

Adding the Union Jack to a Washington-planned military operation has been more significant politically than militarily. It has enabled the American government to show that it was acting in the common interest of more countries than just itself. Tony Blair was so enamoured of building up a close personal relationship with Bill Clinton and George W. Bush that he became popular in America and lost popularity in Britain by sending British troops to war in Iraq on a false premise minted in Washington (Chilcot, 2016; Naughtie, 2004).

A transactional relationship. The security relationship between the United States and the United Kingdom is transactional rather than unconditional. It depends on the convergence of the national interests of the two countries. For example, when the UK used military force to seize the Suez Canal from Egypt in 1956, American opposition quickly led to the independent British mission being abandoned. When President Johnson pressed Prime Minister Harold Wilson to commit British troops to the Vietnam war, Wilson successfully resisted sending troops to join American forces in fighting in a lost cause.

The American view of Britain's in-and-out relationship with the European Union has been transactional. While the United States had a limited direct interest in the EU, it welcomed British membership as providing North Atlantic balance to the narrower continental outlook of many EU member states. This encouraged President de Gaulle vetoing British membership in the EU as threatening to undermine its European character. Britain's departure from the European Union did not directly affect relations between Westminster and Washington. The chief impact has been the shattering of the Brexiters' illusion that the United States would accept a free-trade agreement on terms that met British interests but not American in fields such as agriculture. Five rounds of negotiations led to no deal; talks stopped in October 2020.

The tilt of the United States to the Pacific has led Washington to identify China as a super-power challenger to the United States in Asia. While this view is shared in London, the UK remains sidelined when major decisions are taken in Washington and Beijing. A specific trilateral defence relationship has been created between the United Kingdom, the United States and Australia, institutionalized as AUKUS. The Anglo-American countries are giving assistance to Australia in developing nuclear-powered submarines to contribute to its security. However, this does not mean that the UK or Australia has the military force to match that of the United States in a confrontation with China.

The UK: An island linked with many continents

Although geographers may classify the UK as a peripheral part of the European continent, British politicians have used its insular position and naval force as a means to create a presence on distant continents. When almost a quarter of the world's map was coloured pink to show territories that were part of the British Empire, only a minuscule part of the European continent was included.

Gibraltar and Malta were valued as defending sea routes that led to the Suez Canal and India. The English Channel protected Britain from Europe, while the Channel Tunnel has made Europe very accessible from London. Relations with the Commonwealth and the United States have fallen in significance, but Europe has continued to loom large, Brexit or no Brexit.

The English Channel as a drawbridge. While the English Channel separates Britain from Europe by as little as 20 miles, this was sufficient to stop the German blitzkrieg that in 1940 quickly conquered the countries opposite England's Channel coast. Pulling up the drawbridge across the Channel could not protect British cities from aerial bombardment by the German Luftwaffe. The Channel did provide protection from invasion by the German Army while parts of Europe and the Soviet Union suffered as a battleground. Britain was also free of the taint of collaboration with Nazi Germany, which in occupied Europe tainted some individual politicians and national regimes as collaborators with the Nazis.

The Western approach to Britain became vital to military victory in the Second World War because it was the path for American ships carrying war supplies, food and troops from across the Atlantic to British ports. While the ports were more difficult for the Luftwaffe to reach, the Atlantic was a hunting ground for German submarines. The creation of the North Atlantic Treaty Organisation in 1949 institutionalized the Western approaches as the principal link in Britain's defence. A history of mutual trust between the British and American military, security officials and diplomats has created a British understanding of its place in North Atlantic Europe that is much greater than its understanding of its place in continental Europe.

Mental barriers to Europe go down and up. British prime ministers kept at a distance from the establishment of European institutions on both economic and cultural grounds. Since Britain had not been invaded and a battleground, its industrial economy was able to operate flat out rather than take years to reconstruct; its chief trading partners were on other continents; and a Labour government that had nationalized British industries had no wish to see them Europeanized. Conservatives wanted to reduce national regulations on the economy rather than add European regulations. The inability of Europeans to defend themselves re-enforced a cultural belief that they are 'not like us' and 'Britain is best'.

The recognition of difficulties in the British economy led Harold Macmillan to request a place in the European Economic Community. The third request by Edward Heath succeeded in gaining entry in 1973 (Section 3.3). In keeping with her free-market principles, Margaret Thatcher succeeded in reducing barriers within the EEC to create a Single Europe Market, from which she over-optimistically assumed Britain would specially benefit. While the EU became and remains Britain's biggest market for exports, EU imports to the UK are larger, albeit much smaller than trade between countries within the Single Europe Market. When Jacques Delors turned the single market into a market with continental social and economic regulations that were legally binding in Britain, the British government opted out of the European Monetary Union and further steps towards European integration.

While public opinion about the state of Britain has fluctuated, Britons have consistently tended to feel positive towards other old Commonwealth countries on other continents. For example, a YouGov poll (2020) found that four-fifths of respondents were positive about Australia, New Zealand and Canada. The top-rated European country, Spain, is a tourist destination not a political partner. Just over half of YouGov respondents rate France and Germany positively.

The 2016 referendum on whether Britain should remain or leave the European Union showed politicians had only a foggy understanding of the European Union and no political desire to learn facts that were contrary to their domestic foreign policy. David Cameron acted as if good personal relationships with select European leaders could gain concessions that would reduce EU influence on British policies and convince Eurosceptics to vote in favour of remaining in the EU. He did not realize that the EU's *acquis communautaire* would not allow a member state to renegotiate policies that they had previously accepted. The referendum outcome showed the UK was divided: a narrow majority voted to leave the EU and a big minority voted to remain.

As soon as the Brexit vote was known, European Union leaders defined their goal – the maintenance of the authority and membership of a 27-state EU. The negotiating principle that flowed from this was that Britain should not be allowed to cherry-pick, that is, keep the economic advantages, it had while a EU member and becoming free of the obligations to which member states were bound (Barnier, 2021). The EU's position explicitly rejected Boris

Johnson's 'cake' strategy for Brexit, keeping the benefits of membership and avoiding its costs. Negotiations of British prime ministers with Brussels about the UK's relationship with the EU after it withdrew failed to take account of the relative power of the two parties in the negotiations.

David Cameron's replacement as prime minister, Theresa May, sought to appease Tory MPs expecting instant withdrawal by promptly giving notice to the EU that the UK would leave the EU, an action that imposed a two-year time limit on negotiations for the post-Brexit relationship. This deadline weakened the bargaining position of London, because it meant that if no agreement could be reached, the UK would lose the advantages that membership conferred in dealing with countries that were by far its biggest trading partner. This would create a so-called hard Brexit in which the UK would lose far more than European countries.

Both Theresa May and Boris Johnson pursued a domestic negotiating policy that sought to create a parliamentary majority in favour of a UK-EU agreement with Brussels. This was needed to offset the defection of Tory MPs who favoured keeping close to the EU with the votes of Labour MPs in favour of withdrawal. On fifteen votes a cross-party majority of MPs voted down a variety of measures put forward by the government or opponents to its plans for the UK's post-Brexit relations with the European Union (Martill, 2023; Rose, 2021: 196).

When Boris Johnson became prime minister, he mistakenly thought that the EU needed an agreement as much or more than the UK. He threatened that if not given concessions, Britain would leave the EU without any agreement. The EU treated this as a suicidal British option and refused concessions. In the event, it was Britain that had to make concessions. Boris Johnson's party won the December 2019 general election with the slogan 'Get Brexit done'; this finally produced a parliamentary majority for a withdrawal agreement between the EU and the UK. It imposed harsher conditions on the UK than those that MPs had previously rejected. Johnson subsequently declared that the UK had the right to ignore (others called it renege on) terms that Britain had signed up to that were against Britain's interest.

On the day that Britain left the European Union the French President Emmanuel Macron commented, 'You may be leaving the EU but you are not leaving Europe'. Having inherited maximum political distrust in Brussels,

Prime Minister Rishi Sunak sought to restore diplomatic relations with the EU. The frictions resulting from the anomalous position of Northern Ireland in trade with Great Britain were revised in the 2023 Windsor Agreement. It reduced the operational friction that Brexit placed on trade between these two parts of the UK, which do not exist between Northern Ireland and the Republic, a European Union member state.

The Brexit Withdrawal Agreement makes provision for reviewing the operation of economic relations between Britain and the European Union in 2025. It does not alter the EU's overriding principle of not giving non-member states exceptional treatment that could disadvantage its member states. Sir Keir Starmer initially said he wanted to use the review to get a better deal for Britain. However, he has since changed his rhetoric to endorse making Brexit work, for fear that stressing advantages of cooperation with Brussels would unleash a flood of Conservative claims that he was subverting the majority result of the 2016 vote to leave the EU. This has discouraged Labour politicians from developing a strategy that would mutually benefit both Britain and the EU. Thus, after a meeting between Labour politicians and the EU Ambassador to Britain, an EU staff member noted, 'They don't seem to know what they were saying' (Shipman, 2024; *Economist*, 2024).

From the perspective of Brussels, the UK is no longer a part of Europe but a third country, a term describing non-member states on other continents. This is consistent with the claim of Boris Johnson that withdrawal from the EU would give the government the freedom to create a global Britain advancing the security, prosperity and sovereignty of the UK (HM Government, 2021: 13). However, these very general goals leave open where specifically the UK fits in an interdependent world (Rose, 2021: 225ff).

The UK nonetheless maintains a major political presence in international affairs. It holds one of five permanent seats in the Security Council of the United Nations, it is on the governing bodies of the World Bank and the International Monetary Fund and a significant number of their economists have degrees from British universities. It is a member of the G-7 Group of major liberal democracies and market economies. Informal links with the American government give British officials contacts not available to countries such as France. Historical ties with old and new Commonwealth states provide links with many developing countries across continents. These institutional ties are managed through a sophisticated Foreign, Commonwealth and Development Office, albeit a ministry that has suffered significant cuts in its resources.

War returns in the near abroad

For decades the British government has given priority to international economic policies as the primary means of maintaining its security, defending the foreign exchange value of the pound, promoting trade links and giving foreign aid to developing countries. A year before the war in Ukraine broke out, HM Government (2021) set out an ambitious foreign and security policy. Promoting science and technology and an open international order were the leading priorities. Strengthening security at home came third. The Russian invasion of Ukraine in 2022 gave an unexpected and unwanted reminder that Britain is too close for comfort to a European continent where Russia is an active aggressor. HM Government (2023) refreshed its policy, now described as *Responding to a More Contested and Volatile World*. Rishi Sunak's foreword stated:

> The security and prosperity of the Euro-Atlantic will remain our core priority, bolstered by a reinvigoration of our European relationships. But that cannot be separated from our wider neighbourhood on the periphery of our continent and a free and open Indo-Pacific. We will deepen relationships, support sustainable development and poverty alleviation, and tackle shared challenges including climate change.

Maintaining more than half a dozen priorities around the world requires giving increased spending on military defence priority over increased spending on popular domestic programmes. It requires urgent action, for Russia has demonstrated that it has both the military resources and political will to act aggressively on short notice, and consistency is needed to implement long-term plans for developing new weapons and forces. Since 2012 the Ministry of Defence has published a dozen plans and had seven Secretaries of State. Keir Starmer has pledged the Labour government will increase public spending on defence to 2.5 percent of GDP 'as soon as resources allow'.

A rundown military force. From the start of the Second World War until 1963, Britain maintained a large armed force based on the conscription of able-bodied men to serve in uniform for two years. At the end of the war in 1945, there were 4.5 million in uniform and conscription kept the forces above 250,000 plus reserves for two decades. Armed insurrections by nationalists seeking to hasten their country's independence from the British Empire kept the British military active on three continents for more than a decade after the Second World War. Concurrently, Britain developed nuclear weapons as a second-strike deterrent against attack by a nuclear power, that is, the Soviet Union and now Russia.

The end of conscription reduced the number in uniform to 176,000 in 1970, and the size of the force has been reduced since. The 2010 Strategic Defence and Security Review recommended a cut of 40,000 in personnel and a significant cut in defence spending too. By 2018 the armed forces were one-third the size when conscription ended and the number in the military reserve had fallen by three-quarters. When the war in Ukraine broke out the army was thousands short of its authorized number of recruits. This made the British Army smaller than it was two hundred years earlier.

In the past half-century artillery, tanks, planes and ships that military forces require have become increasingly sophisticated and expensive and time-consuming and uncertain to produce. As a country with a substantial high-technology sector, Britain has the capacity to design high technology military equipment, as was demonstrated in developing radar and jet engines. However, these developments occurred when the government made their development an unqualified priority.

The procurement of new armoured vehicles, planes and ships is subject to significant delays and cost over-runs. The National Audit Office (2023) review of the ten-year programme of weapons procurement, which accounts for almost half the Ministry of Defence budget, concluded that it is 'unaffordable'. A year later the House of Commons Public Accounts Committee (2024: 3) declared that it was disappointed but not surprised that the multi-billion pound gap between defence spending and what is needed to support government policies had risen to a record high and programmes were delayed and costs overrun.

Even though the British government meets the NATO target of spending two per cent of GDP on defence, a disproportionate amount is devoted to nuclear weapons to deter a missile attack on Britain but of no use in defending on land a NATO country invaded by Russia. To maintain an effective military force requires the commitment of substantial resources that can be put into action on short notice if a threat to security arises. While Britain's military resources are much greater than the big majority of European countries, they are no match for Russia. On other continents, its resources are limited to a supporting political role to action by the United States, for example, in countering the attack of Houthi terrorists on merchant shipping in the Persian Gulf.

Britain and Ukraine. Since the outbreak of the war in Ukraine does not call for the engagement of British troops, the government has been able to play a visible political role in supporting Ukraine. Before the war broke out it sided with the United States in exposing Russia as preparing for aggression while French and German leaders attempted to talk Vladimir Putin out of invading Ukraine. Once war broke out, Prime Minister Boris Johnson was the first national leader to fly to Kyiv to show political support, a measure that played to his domestic political advantage, too.

Britain has given much more military and economic aid to Ukraine than France. While Germany has given more economic aid than Britain, it has been more hesitant in delivering military aid to Ukraine. British industries also have a significant capacity to produce military supplies, albeit withdrawal from the EU creates obstacles to exporting supplies to European countries. With Nordic and Baltic states, the UK is part of a 'minilateral' Joint Expeditionary Force that co-ordinates defence on the northern flank of Europe, where the British isles guard the sea link between the United States and Nordic and Baltic countries and a British Major General is in charge of its military co-ordination.

In formulating economic sanctions against Russia, Britain has a major role because London is an important global financial centre and sterling a major international currency. Moreover, many rich Russians have been attracted to London as a place to buy homes and even football clubs. Sanctions can freeze assets of the Russian state banked in London and affect Russians who have become rich through their political connections. However, there is no evidence that this has had an effect on Vladimir Putin's military strategy or personal wealth.

Because the UK is no longer a member of the European Union, its support for Ukraine is done on a bilateral basis with Kyiv. It is therefore not required to sit in meetings about how to help Ukraine with twenty-seven other countries, differing in how much or how little support should be given Ukraine. Nor is it expected to send funds to Brussels that can be credited to the European Union when given to Ukraine. When the time comes to aid the post-war reconstruction of Ukraine, the EU and its member states will take the lead in providing funds for a country that is a potential member. London hopes to play a significant role in financing private sector investment in Ukraine, preferably guaranteed by a European authority, and the British government expects to provide some aid for reconstructing Ukraine.

The return of Donald Trump to the White House would be bad news for Britain, with Sir Keir Starmer, a Labour prime minister in Downing Street. The doubt that Trump has cast on the United States honouring its treaty commitment to defend Europe has already revived the idea of a European Defence Force that was rejected by France in 1954. While Britain's armed force is less than British military commanders would like, it is superior to Germany and more politically trustworthy than that of France. As an island in the North Atlantic, it is not easily reached by Russian troops and its nuclear weapons provide a deterrent against a Russian air attack. If and when the exigencies of national security encourage European countries to form a collective defence force, Britain's relative military strength could play an important role, as it did a century ago. Meanwhile, the military security of a global Britain depends on decisions taken in Moscow and Washington.

Bibliography

Ashton, Nigel J., 2005. 'Harold Macmillan and the "Golden Days" of Anglo-American Relations Revisited, 1957–63'. *Diplomatic History*, 29, 4, 691–723.

Barnier, Michel, 2021. *My Secret Brexit Diary*. Cambridge: Polity Press.

Blair, Tony, 1998. *The Third Way: New Politics for the New Century*. London: Fabian Society Pamphlet No. 588.

Chilcot, Sir John, 2016. *The Report of the Iraq Inquiry: Executive Summary*. London: House of Commons Report 264.

Economist, The, 2024. 'Ever Closer? How Does the EU View the Prospect of Labour Government?' London, 3 February, 21.

Gowing, Margaret, 1974. *Independence and Deterrence: Britain and Atomic Energy, 1945–52*. London: Macmillan, vol. 1.

HM Government, 2021. *Global Britain in a Competitive Age*. London: House of Commons Command Paper 403.

HM Government, 2023. *Responding to a More Contested and Volatile World*. London: House of Commons Command Paper 811.

House of Commons Committee of Public Accounts, 2024. *MoD Equipment Plan 2023–2033*. London: House of Commons Report HC 451.

Martill, Benjamin, 2023. 'Withdrawal Symptoms: Party Factions, Political Change and British Foreign Policy Post-Brexit'. *Journal of European Public Policy*, 30, 11, 2468–91.

National Audit Office, 2023. *The Equipment Plan, 2023–2033: Ministry of Defence*. London: House of Commons Paper 315.

Naughtie, James, 2004. *The Accidental American: Tony Blair and the Presidency*. London: Macmillan.

Prime Minister, 2021. *Global Britain in a Competitive Age. The Integrated Review of Security, Defence, Development and Foreign Policy*. London: Her Majesty's Stationery Office, CP 403.

Rose, Richard, 2021. *How Referendums Challenge European Democracy: Brexit and Beyond*. London: Palgrave Macmillan.

Shipman, Tim, 2024. 'New Deals with Brussels'. *Sunday Times*, 10 March.

Smith, Michael, 2022. *The Real Special Relationship: The True Story of How the British and US Secret Services Work Together*. London: Simon and Schuster.

YouGov, 2020. 'New Zealand Britons' Favourite Country'. London. yougov.co.uk/travel/articles/32688-new-zealand-britons-favourite-country.

Index